CASTLES IN THE AIR

A FAMILY MEMOIR OF LOVE AND LOSS

By Alison Ripley Cubitt
and Molly Ripley

Castles in the Air
Copyright © 2015 by Alison Ripley Cubitt & MD Ripley

The moral rights of the author have been asserted.
All Rights Reserved.

No part of this publication may be reproduced, stored in a retrieval system, or transmitted, in any form or by any means, without the prior permission in writing of the author

Published by Lambert Nagle Media, Winchester, UK
All enquiries to info@lambertnagle.com

This work is registered with the UK Copyright Service

ISBN: 978-0-9933183-1-3

CONTENTS

Introduction	1
PART 1 1937–1944	5
Chapter 1 – An Intriguing Job Offer	7
Chapter 2 – Travels to the South China Sea	13
Chapter 3 – A New Life in Hong Kong	28
Chapter 4 – Fortress Singapore	35
Chapter 5 – In the Shadow of War	43
Chapter 6 – Escape from Colombo	52
Chapter 7 – Castles in the Air	77
Chapter 8 – Reunited in East Africa	95
Chapter 9 – Take a Bow, Mr Stephens	117
Chapter 10 – On His Majesty's Secret Service	136
PART 2 1945–1967	153
Chapter 11 – Nurse Lambert	155
Chapter 12 – The Emergency	165
Chapter 13 – Boarding School	176
Chapter 14 – A Brief Encounter	190
PART 3 1968–2015	203
Chapter 15 – In God's Country	205
Chapter 16 – Spiral	214
Chapter 17 – Family Life	220
Chapter 18 – Death in Paradise	236
About the Author	255
Acknowledgements	257

INTRODUCTION

It was the Christmas holidays, 1967, and I was newly released from boarding school. On the train up to London I was a right pest, questioning my mother non-stop. Would we see the chimps at London Zoo? Feed pigeons in Trafalgar Square? Look at all the lovely shop windows? I must have driven the poor passengers in our carriage mad with my incessant chatter, but unlike most eight-year-olds, I only got to see my mum a couple of times a year. My parents were expats, living and working in Malaysia, while we three children went to school, far away in England.

Mum, known as Molly, was forty-one, small, dark-haired and petite, and had always looked young for her age. We arrived at Victoria Station where we were met by the man we children knew as 'Uncle Steve' who drove us to his flat in South Kensington. If we did go to the zoo or the shops that day, I've since forgotten.

We had two 'Uncle Steves', neither of them related to us. English Uncle Steve was in his late fifties – impeccably turned out in a trench coat and a trilby that covered his receded hairline. He was kind-hearted and well-meaning, but without a family of his own, didn't know how to behave around children. My sister and I held firm opinions about Steve. I once stuck my nose enthusiastically into a rose, eager to inhale the delicate perfume, only to be ticked off in case a bee flew out and stung me. What a spoilsport he was. If you'd asked Susan, who was then twelve, why she

1

too didn't like him, I doubt she could have told you why. A talented pianist, Steve had even offered to leave her his baby grand piano in his will. She felt too embarrassed to accept this gift, and even though she understood that it was extremely generous of him, she asked Mum to tell him no.

Steve lived at Flat No 2, 19 Sumner Place. A mansion flat inside a Georgian building, it had high ceilings and large rooms. In pride of place in the spacious drawing room was the grand piano. On the cream walls were framed landscape paintings, hung in orderly rows. Books and sheet music were hidden away in a cabinet. Everything was neat, tidy and carefully arranged, but to my childish eyes it didn't look much like a home. When we got there, Mum told me that she and Steve needed to have a talk and I was left to my own devices in the kitchen.

I must have got bored as I wandered off, peering into the various rooms. I knew not to touch anything, but there was nothing in that apartment that aroused my curiosity anyway, apart from the low murmur of Mum and Steve talking. I went and stood outside the door, which was ajar – they must have forgotten to close it properly, trying but failing to hear what was being said. As I stood there, glued to the floor, I saw Mum and Steve kissing each other, locked in a loving embrace.

In my head, I was yelling at them to stop: this was wrong. All I knew was that grown-ups weren't meant to behave this way. Here was Mum, clinging to a man we children had always been told to call 'Uncle', while my father was thousands of miles away, working long hours to support his family. Uncle Steve, it seemed to my childish self, was trying to take my father's place. And that seemed so unfair. (It wasn't until I was an adult that I learnt the word for the way I felt: betrayed.) I knew I needed to tell someone, but the someone I wanted to tell, I wasn't going to be seeing for four months. And so I stored this memory for later and made my mind up there and then that whatever secret my mother had, I wasn't going to be part of it. Now that I have dug deeper into my mother's story, I know that she and Steve were saying goodbye. That moment now seems so desperately sad. Molly had known Steve for nearly thirty years and she was breaking the news that we were moving permanently, far across the world to New Zealand.

As I grew older, I began to question myself. Is an eight-year-old a reliable witness? And after Mum's death in 1992, I used her legacy to explore this notion further at film school. I dramatised that secret I'd seen as a child in a *Brief Encounter* style short film, *Waves/Day Return*. My collaborator, Polish director Maciej Pisarek, retained the heart of the story, even though he changed the setting and the era. Our film was screened and won awards at film festivals in Europe, Russia and the USA.

Writing this screenplay and reflecting further led me to ask what hold this man really had over my mother. And what other secrets was she hiding? I hoped that the answer lay in her letters and diaries. In 1988, she sat down to write her memoirs, and in 1990, the last year Mum had written a diary, the entry for 11 November (written on a plane from Singapore to London) reads: *Met interesting Australian lady – SAYS I SHOULD WRITE MY BOOK.*

Much of her memoir had already been written. She'd been writing since her teens. As a professional researcher and writer, I knew I could piece together the story, but did I have the courage? By doing so, would I reveal uncomfortable truths about my mother Molly's seemingly ordinary life?

To begin Molly's story we need to turn the clock back to 1937 when she was eleven and the family were preparing to leave England for a life-changing adventure in the Far East.

PART 1
1937–1944

CHAPTER 1
–AN INTRIGUING JOB OFFER

Molly's horizons stretched from Ireland, where she had family, to France which she could see from the beach at Deal on the Kent coast. She lived there with her fox terrier, Cindy, her father Eric and her mother Hannah, who everyone knew as Don and Ciss.

Nearly forty, Don Lambert was nearing the end of his commission and was soon to be jobless. He had been in the services all his adult life and had neither a profession nor a trade to fall back on. Unemployment was fifteen per cent in 1937. He couldn't have picked a worse year to try to find a new job if he'd tried.

Don had no inherited money and was prepared to do whatever it took to support his young family. His people were humble agricultural workers from Pilton in Somerset, his father was a brewer's cellarman, but a generation later, his daughter Molly would be at an expensive boarding school. By the age of thirteen Don had already left school. The eldest son, he had no choice but to go out to work. His four brothers and sisters needed to be fed and clothed, and on his father's paltry wage, there simply wasn't enough money.

Had he been born a generation earlier, Don would have lived, worked and died in his home village. It was the First

World War which changed my family's future. Don was the type of person who seized opportunities, even if it meant moving away. He joined the Royal Navy at eighteen as a Royal Marine in the Light Infantry: Plymouth Division. On his enlistment form, he gave his occupation as a dairyman. The navy was unusual as it allowed men from humble backgrounds to rise up the ranks if they were good enough, as Admiral Lord Nelson had done. Don was promoted four times to become an NCO (non-commissioned officer).

Don's ship sailed into port at Cork, where he met and fell in love with an Irish girl with blonde hair so long that she could sit on it. Hannah Maria Cecilia Finnie – Ciss – was the youngest of five children. According to the 1911 census, Hannah, then eight, had been living in a tiny terrace house at 18 Harbour View, Queenstown (Cobh) with her father John, fifty, and her mother Hannah, forty-three. Ciss had three brothers: Alexander, seventeen, Michael, sixteen and Francis, eleven. Her sister Mary, the eldest, was eighteen. John Finnie was a ship's rigger, Alexander a shipwright's apprentice, Mary, known as May, a domestic servant, and Michael a boy labourer.

Ireland was at that time undergoing intense political upheaval over Home Rule. The Finnies were devout Irish Catholics, yet John had had to go to England to find work and three of his children had been born there. The struggle to earn enough money to support the children left the family little time for politics. And they must have been cautious about what an independent Ireland might mean for a family struggling to make ends meet; it's possible they felt loyalty towards the British Empire that had provided them with a living.

Don, an Englishman but crucially a Catholic, was welcomed into the family home. Don and Ciss were married in Cork on 2 June 1924, two years after Ireland succeeded in overthrowing its colonial masters to become the Irish Free

State. Ciss left Ireland and moved to Stonehouse Barracks in Plymouth, Devon, next to the Devonport dockyards where Don's Royal Marines unit was based. From the waterfront, the views down the estuary and out to sea must have reminded Ciss of the home town she'd left behind in Ireland.

(Additional photographs, including Figure 1.1, Molly aged nineteen months can be viewed in the gallery section of the website: http://www.lambertnagle.com)

Mary Dorothy, known as Molly, was born on 1 May 1926. When she was just a toddler, Don was sent away to sea for a year, leaving Ciss on her own to care for their young daughter, but when he was home on leave they made the most of their time together, taking to the road on the family motorbike, Ciss and Molly squeezing into the tiny sidecar. The Lamberts had moved twice by the time Molly was eleven, firstly to Wimbledon and then to Deal. They belonged to a close-knit community of fellow Royal Marines and Royal Navy families, many of whom were Catholic. They attended the same church and sent their children to the same schools.

The Lamberts weren't the only family in 1937 facing the end of a naval commission. Many of their friends were in the same predicament. Up in London at Admiralty House, government officials had been keeping a watchful eye on these same naval officers. They were looking to recruit ex-RN and ex-Royal Marines for a job so secret that all they were prepared to reveal was that it involved an overseas posting. Officers with large families were quietly weeded out as it would cost too much to move them all. As well as an outstanding service record, the Admiralty was looking for strength of character, courage, discretion and, above all, the ability to keep secrets.

Don travelled up to London with his colleagues, all of similar age and experience. He must have felt anxious with so much riding on the outcome, but to do well at the interview, he had to push his anxiety aside.

On the train home Don travelled with an air of excitement and anticipation. The first interview had gone well. Now it was a question of waiting. Weeks later, the letter finally arrived inviting Don to a further round of interviews, aptitude assessments, fitness tests and medicals, followed by another agonising wait for a decision to be made.

By the summer, job offers for the Lamberts, as well as the Carvers, Coopers and Townsends, had finally come through. Don was offered a civilian role with the Admiralty based in Hong Kong, the British colony next to China. He was being asked to take a leap into the unknown, half-way across the world, with his family in tow. Would they be prepared to take up a new life abroad, far away from loved ones? One way or another, the future would involve a major upheaval.

Don was permitted to discuss the pros and cons of accepting the job with Ciss and the other families, but only in private. Once they'd made the decision, there could be no turning back. If there was an emergency back in England, it would take five weeks to get home. Ciss, who was seemingly quiet and reserved, had proved her resilience by leaving Ireland to live in England. And she wasn't the complaining sort. As the families talked late into the night, they were faced with a stark choice: take the job abroad or stay in England and face an uncertain future. It was a unanimous decision. A job offer like this was too good to turn down.

Don and Ciss broke the news to Molly, having to get out the map to show her where Hong Kong was. She had mixed emotions: excited to be going, sad that her beloved dog couldn't go with them, and cheered by the fact her close friends Daphne Carver and Yseult Cooper were going too. She began to look forward to this new adventure.

Don had been recruited for the Far East Combined

Bureau, FECB, part of the Government Code and Cypher School (GC&CS). After the First World War, the Royal Navy, under the command of the Admiralty, had taken over responsibility for signals intelligence. They had uncovered a major Japanese spy network in Singapore and had set up the FECB in Hong Kong, which was strategically placed to monitor Japanese, Chinese and Russian intelligence and radio traffic. Japan, even then, was the greatest threat as it had invaded China and withdrawn from the League of Nations.

As Michael Smith in *The Emperor's Codes* describes it, the spying operation in Hong Kong ran an intelligence reporting section, a wireless intercept station, and a code-breaking section, where Don would be based. He would be working alongside Japanese interpreters and naval officers, intercepting and deciphering Japanese naval signals and messages. Don's job title was Pensioner Clerk, giving no clue whatsoever about what he really did for a living.

During the Second World War, GC & CS was based at Bletchley Park. In the film, *The Imitation Game*, Alan Turing and his team at Bletchley try to crack the German Enigma machine. German codes and ciphers were sent in International Morse Code, using the letters of the common Latin alphabet, but Japanese Morse Code, or Wabun, was entirely different and had to be painstakingly learnt from scratch. Wabun code represented Japanese Kanji characters, which would require a skilled Japanese translator. And then, of course, the code-breakers had to work out the meaning of the decoded and translated English words. It was a monotonous job, requiring the utmost concentration and attention to detail.

In July 1937, as the codes and cipher clerks were training to take up their jobs in Hong Kong, two mighty armies were exchanging fire near Peking. A Japanese soldier had gone missing, and Japanese troops forced their way into town, determined to find him, accusing the Chinese of taking him prisoner. But the soldier was merely lovelorn and had gone in search of female company.

Neither side would back down. Known as the China Incident, this was all the excuse that both sides needed to start what became the second Sino-Japanese War. If news of this war made the codes and cipher clerks uneasy, it was too late to back out.

Ciss and Don were so preoccupied with the move, there can't have been time for second thoughts anyway. Don had to travel up to London every day for further training, so it was Ciss who planned the logistics. She arranged the passports, packed up the house and their belongings, and sold off large pieces of furniture. Much to Molly's sorrow, her dog, Cindy, had to be given away to friends. In what little spare time they had left, they went on goodbye visits to relatives. Ciss's older sister, May, came to see them off at Tilbury docks. Although May and Ciss weren't close, it must have been a difficult goodbye not knowing when they would see each other again.

Having made the decision to go, Don just wanted to get on with it and put his newly learnt knowledge of codes and ciphers to good use. Although he was impatient to start his new job, he was also determined to keep himself busy on their five-week voyage to Hong Kong. To break the monotony of the enforced holiday, he wrote a log of their journey.

CHAPTER 2
– TRAVELS TO THE SOUTH CHINA SEA

Don Lambert's log of his voyage on the SS *Corfu*

November 19th 1937

Left UJ Hostel [Union Jack Club, affordable lodgings for the armed forces and their families] at 9am for Liverpool Street. May accompanied us and Les and Florence [Don's brother and wife] came to see us off.

I was struck by the number of Lascars [Indian sailors] awaiting the Boat Train, their brightly coloured turbans giving a splash of colour to the dingy scene. We left Tilbury at about 1pm and we had a last sight of May, Les and Florence waving on the jetty.

The trip to Southampton was calm. Molly seems to have caught a touch of 'flu and she is confined to her cabin. Had three goodbye telegrams from Win [Don's sister] and the Admiralty. Passed Deal about 6pm. Thought of old Bert Prior, etc.

November 20th

Arrived Southampton at 4am. Weather still quite clear and sea calm. Molly still very 'seedy' and we left her in bed until

5pm. Ciss went ashore to do some shopping and bought a thermometer, Aspro, etc. I went ashore when she returned to post some letters and get some books.

Sailed at 4pm. We stayed on deck until we had cleared the harbour, getting one last look at England for a long time, I expect. Headed down Channel. This is a most comfortable ship and there is very little motion on her as yet.

November 21st

Passed Ushant [island in the English Channel near France] at 4am and we are now in the Bay of Biscay. We are rolling a bit, but it is a steady motion. In spite of this many people are sea-sick. Molly is much better today, though she has been a trifle sick. Ciss also feeling it a little. Deck games have commenced and I managed to get a game of deck quoits. Molly is also joining in now and beginning to settle down.

Weather began to deteriorate in the afternoon with rain squalls and a few white horses on the sea. In the sun it is beautiful. Passed many ships homeward bound.

November 22nd

Cleared Bay of Biscay at 4am. Ship rolls a little in a ground swell. Played deck quoits in the morning, bridge in the afternoon and deck tennis in the evening. Molly is much better and having a good time on deck. She has made friends with some children going to Hong Kong, but the ship is very dull from the point of view of organised games. Hope it bucks up soon. There is rumoured to be a dance tonight, but I doubt it.

There have been a few heavy rain squalls today and the sky looks very stormy.

November 23rd

Tangier looks a very pretty place from the sea. The weather was very beautiful and the air delightfully balmy [yet] it is the middle of November. The Moors are very picturesque and many of them come round the ship selling fancy leather goods.

We sailed for Gibraltar after an hour and the first sight of the Rock was awe-inspiring. The top was covered in mist. We went ashore at 1.30pm until 5pm, and Ciss and Molly were thrilled with the strange sights and customs. We found cigarettes and silk amazingly cheap and bought a few things, then sailed at 6.30pm for Marseilles. The view from the ship is delightful, the lights on the Rock making it look like fairyland. Scavenger Hunt [a popular children's game] in evening. Weather beautiful.

November 24th

At sea on our way from Gibraltar to Marseilles. Weather beautiful and everyone blossomed out into summer clothes. Played bridge in forenoon, deck tennis and deck quoits in afternoon. Had a yarn [chat] to a Yank on board and he began to get a bit 'uppish' so have decided to leave him alone. After dinner the ship's band played dance music until 11pm. Ciss and Molly were thrilled with their first experience of dancing at sea.

November 25th

Weather got up a bit during the night, and by 8am it was blowing a 60 miles per hour gale from the North West. A lot of people are sea-sick. Played deck tennis and quoits during forenoon until it got a bit too rough.

Arrived at Marseilles at 4pm and we got quite a thrill. We were stopped in the harbour waiting for the pilot when a big Turkish cargo boat came very close. When she was very nearly on top of us she let go her cable, but the wind caught her and a collision seemed inevitable. She missed our stern by about a foot.

We anchored and remained in the harbour until 4am. Apparently we are waiting for the gale to abate. Played Tombola in the evening. Great fun. Many more people lined up than I expected.

November 26th

Awoke to find the ship tied up to the side. Terrific clamour. These French men are terribly vociferous.

[In Marseille there was time for sightseeing including a visit to the church of Notre Dame. Don admired the interior and the view from the top of the cliff, but didn't find much else of interest].

November 27th

Left Marseilles at 4am. Weather still fairly good, though there is rather a heavy swell. Played deck tennis and Rummy in forenoon. Everyone seems rather quiet and we spent the afternoon in deck chairs on deck. Had a Magic Lantern show in our cabin in the evening. All the kids were very touched. [That evening Don and Ciss went to pre-dinner drinks with passengers leaving the ship.] After dinner there was a dance, but as it was only wireless music it did not go down well. We made up a party and sat in the bar until after midnight having farewell drinks.

November 28th

Awoke to find the ship rolling very heavily. Everyone a bit grim today, too many drinks last night. Too much of a swell to play games so we spend the time on deck, walking and talking. Lazed around in deck chairs all afternoon and kept a look-out for Malta. We arrived after 6pm and Malta looked very pretty in the half light.

It seems as though all the interesting people are getting off here and the ship looks like being very dull from now on. I was elected a member of the sports committee. Sailed for Port Said at 9pm.

November 29th

At sea steaming towards Port Said. Ship rolling like a tub in a ground swell. She really is a very bad ship for rolling, but I am told she is better in a really rough sea than in a swell. It was very funny at lunch. She gave a lurch and hurled chairs, plates and everything else across the dining saloon.

Managed to get in some games of deck quoits, deck tennis, bucket quoits, etc., all practice for the tournament.

Tried to change our cabin for one a deck higher. No luck yet, but we *may* be able to do so after Port Said.

Nothing much doing at night so we stick around in the lounge playing a lot of silly games. Finished up by playing 'Coffee Pot' [a word guessing game] with the Yanks. Damned silly game.

November 30th

Weather fairly good. Spent most of forenoon working on a dance programme for Friday. Also arranged a Whist Drive to take place tonight. Spent most of the afternoon on deck playing various games. [At this point in the voyage Don complains about the monotony of days spent at sea.] In the evening played Poker with the Yanks until 7.30pm. We arrive at Port Said at 5am, and we want to go ashore to get some Xmas cards which must be posted in Aden.

December 1st

Awoke to find the ship tied up at Port Said. Have never been here before and found it most interesting. One gets ashore by means of pontoons attached to the ship. Natives all around the ship were trying to sell their wares. We went ashore and paid a visit to Simon Arzt's. This place looks like Selfridges on a smaller scale. One seems to be able to get anything there and the place never seems to be closed.

The boys doing the 'Gilly Gilly' stuff [children's entertainers who performed tricks] amused Molly immensely, as did the boys diving for pennies. We bought some Xmas cards, etc. in Simon Arzt's and had our photos taken. We sailed again at 10pm, and the scenery going through the Suez was marvellous. We spent nearly all day on deck.

December 2nd

Cleared the Suez about 4am. Steaming through the Red Sea today. Not nearly as warm as I expected. Deck games in full swing. Awnings spread. All stewards gone into whites. What we can see of the coast is flat, brown and uninteresting.

[Spent the] day arranging the Carnival Dance for Monday and writing letters home for Xmas. Swimming bath opened today and Molly has had a fine time in it. [The swimming pool on ships back then was often nothing more than sheets of canvas filled with seawater.] The children gave a concert in the afternoon and Molly did her part very well. She seems to be entirely self-possessed. Tonight it is very warm. The air is hot and sticky.

December 3rd

Still steaming through the Red Sea. There does not seem to be a breath of air anywhere, and the coolest place is the Dining Saloon where we sit near the ventilators. Everyone is wearing shorts and other rigs in an endeavour to keep cool. It must be a hell of a place in the summer. The swimming pool is doing good business and all the deck games are well patronised. The weather is clear and fine and the sea smooth.

Played a few competition games and lost them all. Ciss is doing better in the deck quoits and bill board competitions. Spent quite a lot of time talking to the Yanks, and after dinner the Purser invited us to his cabin for a drink. We stayed there playing the gramophone and drinking until 11.30pm. Finished up with an impromptu dance in the Smoking Room.

December 4th

Still in the Red Sea. A fairly strong head wind. Played deck tennis in the morning and wrote a few letters. We arrive at Aden at 5am tomorrow, and after *that* we can safely say we are on our way to the East. Been busy today writing the Xmas mail. We thought *we* had a lot of letters to get rid of, but one Yank beat the book by buying 350 stamps.

December 5th

Arrived in Aden at 5am. The place looks extremely forbidding from the sea and appears to be nothing but an extinct crater of a volcano. We went ashore at 7am. It seems to be just a sun-baked inferno. We paid a visit to the native quarter and I have never seen so many goats or so many flies. Ciss bought a pair of white shoes here, though there are practically no shops of note. We sailed for Bombay at 10am and, I think, no one was sorry to see the last of Aden.

December 6th

In the Arabian Sea steaming towards Bombay. Weather very nice with a stiff breeze which keeps the temperatures down. Busy most of the day organising the Carnival Dance tonight. Everyone [working] on their costumes. Ciss has borrowed a very nice jockey outfit while Molly looks pretty in her Spanish Dancer costume.

Most people went to dinner in fancy dress. The effect was very picturesque. I did not wear fancy dress but wore a dinner jacket. I was MC of the dance, which went off very well, though it seems difficult to instil any life into some of these people.

December 7th

There were one or two heavy rain squalls during the morning. We paid a visit to the bridge and found it most interesting. Navigation seems almost fool-proof nowadays and I was fascinated by the echo-sounding gear which registers the depth of water. The kiddies held their fancy dress party in the afternoon and presents were distributed from a Xmas tree. Molly recited very well and many people remarked on her fine delivery. I took a few snaps of her and the other children then we had dog-racing after dinner with toy dogs and dice. Weather got up a bit at night and we had to close the shutters.

December 8th

Steaming through the Arabian Sea towards Bombay, where we expect to arrive at 4pm tomorrow. Warm sun and a cooling breeze. Saw many flying fish and porpoises, but have yet [to] see any sharks. Umpired a couple of deck tennis finals, then managed to beat my opponent and get into the semi-finals of singles deck tennis. Shall be glad to get ashore for a few hours. Being at sea all the time gets a trifle monotonous.

Had another dance after dinner tonight. Very good show. It was in the nature of a farewell party for the people who are disembarking at Bombay.

December 9th

Arrived at Bombay at 4pm and tied up alongside Ballard Pier. Bombay looks very impressive from the sea, but, like all Eastern cities, the illusion is rather shattered when one gets ashore. We all went ashore at 5pm and made a few purchases in the Bazaar, then I went ashore alone at 7.45 until 9 pm and had a look round. Not very impressed. Sailed for Colombo at 11pm. Weather beautiful.

* * * *

Molly wrote little in her memoirs about the trip, but she did recall this:

Remember seeing the Rock of Gibraltar. Enjoyed the shipboard trip as I met several nice girls going to Hong Kong, the food (especially the pistachio nut ice creams) and the Fancy Dress party, to which I went as a gypsy. Remember going ashore in Bombay and being terrified and disgusted at the spitting of betel nut juice all over the place. Couldn't wait to get back on the boat again. Dimly remember going ashore at Colombo, Ceylon and how warm and pleasant it was.

I can understand why Molly recalled the food on board ship, as they were served what, in that time of austerity, would have been elaborate meals. Family meals at home would have been simpler: one course, perhaps two at weekends or on special occasions. It must have seemed as though they were going out to dinner every night. A typical adult Tourist Class lunch menu from the sister ship of the *Corfu*, the *Strathmore*, in 1936 consisted of soup or Welsh rarebit to start, followed by veal cutlets with bacon, potatoes served three ways and bringals (aubergine). On the cold sideboard was potted meat and fish, Leicester (pork) pie, roast rib of beef and ox tongue. There was a choice of four salads, including beetroot and American. On the sweets menu was fruit roll pudding and a blackcurrant water ice. The cheese course offered four types of cheese, including gorgonzola, accompanied by a selection of bread rolls.

* * * *

December 12th

Arrived at Colombo at 4am. This looks like a lovely place from the sea: palms and coconut trees growing right down to the water's edge. A big illuminated sign saying 'Ceylon for Best Tea' stands out. We went ashore at 9.30am and went for a drive round the island, visiting Victoria Gardens and Mount Lavinia.

The natives are most friendly, and the cleanliness and good repair of the roads is very noticeable after Bombay and other places we have seen. Ciss bought a tablecloth and some handkerchiefs here. Altogether it was a nice day, though *very* hot.

We sailed for Penang at 6pm and observed a fierce thunderstorm over Colombo as we stood out to sea.

December 13th

At sea steaming towards Penang. Sea calm and seems very hot. Some humourist has destroyed all the competition notices.

Every day seems to get more monotonous and we shall be glad when 23 December comes. Day spent in playing games, sleeping and reading. If we have much more of this inactivity, none of us will *want* to do any more work. Everyone seems a little fed up with themselves these days. The ship is getting more empty every day, and it is difficult to stimulate interest in games, etc. The competitions seem to have entered a period of stalemate, but they must be played off before we reach Penang on Thursday.

Dance at night on shelter deck.

December 14th

Still in Bay of Bengal. Weather is a trifle cooler today with a stiff breeze.

Some rather nasty news from China on the wireless today. Japanese have been firing on British and American gunboats and merchant ships in the Yangtse. Things appear rather grim, but don't think it will come to a show down. [The Japanese sank the USS *Panay* as a deliberate provocation, designed to draw both Britain and the USA into a war. But Don was proved right. Neither Britain nor the USA had the money or appetite to take on Japan in a war in 1937.]

Managed to get to the Xmas finals of the competitions, which will be played tomorrow. Day again spent in reading, playing games and sleeping. Lazy life this. The journey gets more boring every day and all the people on board are getting a bit fed up with each other. Ran a Whist Drive at night but with no luck.

December 15th

Sighted land during the afternoon so we must be nearing Penang. Weather very hot with little breeze. All the sports finals were played off today. I lost in the Deck Tennis Singles finals to Mr Collyer, but it was a good game. Managed to win 2/6 as runner-up.

There was a very heavy thunderstorm in the evening. The lightning flashes were extremely vivid and played all round the ship. We held a dance at night where the sports prizes were distributed. Some of our passengers are disembarking tomorrow and were making whoopee.

December 16th

Arrived at Penang, which looks a very pretty place from the sea, at 4am. We went ashore at 9am and had our first ride in a rickshaw, which amused Molly. Then we went out about 5 miles to see the Waterfall Gardens, a place of great natural beauty. The monkeys, which are quite tame, intrigued Molly very much.

It was blazing hot ashore, and most of the shops appeared to be Chinese and the items in the shops are very dear. There is a very definite Eastern flavour about Penang which gives one the first indication that one is nearing China.

Left Penang for Singapore at 3.30pm.

December 17th

On our way to Singapore. Steaming through land-locked seas. I hear we nearly ran aground just after we left Penang; I knew the engines were stopped for some reason and the water was very muddy. The weather is still beautiful, but last night we ran into a terrific thunderstorm. The rain lashed down; it was so thick that the engines were again stopped as we had lost our bearings. Arrived at Singapore at 3.30pm and the place looks very beautiful from the sea. The coast all around is most beautifully green. A large crowd of English people was on quay to welcome us, but no one whom we knew.

We went ashore before dinner, and again after dinner to see *You Can't Have Everything* [1937 musical with Alice Faye and Don Ameche] at the Capitol.

December 18th

Went ashore in Singapore again in forenoon. This place amazes us with its magnificent buildings. The post office is wonderful, and the roads are far better than those at home. The quaint mixture of two civilisations is very intriguing, for about two-thirds of the population is Chinese. It is certainly the cleanest Eastern city we have found yet. There is much shipping in the harbour, but no signs of any men-of-war.

We lost many passengers here and the ship will be very empty and dull from here to Hong Kong.

We sailed from Singapore on the last lap of our journey at 12 noon. The weather is still quite good, although I hear this [stage] of the [voyage] can be very rough at times. No sign of that yet though. Wonderful moon.

December 19th

At sea, steaming towards Hong Kong. We shall be *very* glad when we arrive, for every day gets more monotonous. Everyone is more or less broke and, with one or two exceptions, the type of passenger left on board is not very exhilarating.

The sea is rather choppy. We are pitching quite a bit. I hear we will arrive in Hong Kong on Wednesday 22nd December at 1pm, for which the Gods be praised. We did a bit of packing and Molly had her final dip today. Packed the cabin trunk, which is something towards it.

No news from China today.

December 20th

Weather has improved somewhat today, and in the cabin it is still very warm.

We spent the morning reading and talking, with a game of deck quoits to break the monotony. We all had our hair cut, etc., but everyone is thoroughly bored. I suppose that is natural after five weeks of idleness.

The wireless news mentions that Britain is considering strengthening her naval forces in the Far East. About time too. I shall be damned glad to get back to work again and to know the boat situation in Hong Kong. Not much longer to wait now.

[If the Japanese army had continued to sweep south through China, Hong Kong, without naval defences, would have been the next casualty. The last thing Britain needed was a war with Japan.]

December 21st

Still a certain amount of swell, which is coming in on the bow so we are not rolling. Ship is pitching a bit though. Decidedly cooler, but still quite comfortable.

We will arrive at Hong Kong at 4pm on 22nd, a day earlier than we anticipated, and we are all very glad. Altered course due north at lunch-time. Now catching the swell on our starboard bow causing the ship to corkscrew, but not badly enough to be uncomfortable.

We did a little more packing so we shall not have a great deal to do tomorrow. Very little doing on board. All counting the hours until our arrival.

December 22nd

Arrived at Hong Kong at 4pm. Our first glimpse of China was the Chinese fishing junks, which we saw on the port side. These vessels fish in pairs with a drag net behind them. They look extremely picturesque with the sun shining on their patchwork sails.

I was disappointed with my first view of Hong Kong. The country looks extremely rocky and barren from the sea.

Somehow I expected to see the green beauty which one experiences approaching Colombo and Singapore.

The harbour, however, is a wonderful sight. We saw the *Asahi Maru* – a big Japanese liner – high and dry on the rocks where she had been blown by the typhoon.

All the Venables were there to meet us. We were *very* pleased to see some homely faces.

And now for a new life – I wonder.

CHAPTER 3
– A NEW LIFE IN HONG KONG

The Lamberts had to organise their own temporary lodgings, so it must have come as an enormous relief to be invited to stay with friends they'd known in Deal. In Hong Kong living space was at a premium, and it was a squeeze to find house room for a couple and a child in a small flat. Molly recalled having to sleep in the same bed as a child who was a bed-wetter. She was very relieved when her parents found a place to rent and they could move into 186b Nathan Road in Kowloon. Their new home was on the first floor of a small two-storey building, above a traditional Chinese shophouse.

Much of Kowloon was still countryside back then. Joyce Fitch, who lived in Hong Kong and attended the same school as Molly, describes Kowloon as she knew it in the 1930s:

There weren't any shops past St Andrew's Church on Nathan Road [although] there was a [picture] theatre up there. I remember going to the pictures very often.

Source: *Christopher De Wolf's blog, Urban Photo*

Kowloon as semi-rural is difficult for me to comprehend. When I travelled to Hong Kong in the 1980s, from the moment I stepped off the plane on a sweltering July day I was overwhelmed by the relentless pace of the city. And all I recall on the taxi ride from the airport was the noise and the traffic jams; angry drivers hooting their horns and shouting and swearing at each other in Cantonese. The old world and the new had met head on in this vertical city, where ever-taller skyscrapers were being built yet the scaffolding was still made out of bamboo. Up until then, I don't think I'd ever been anywhere that crowded.

Not a trace of the old shophouse building at 186 remains today. Currently home to a silk and fabric shop, the road itself is now a two-lane highway.

Rona Morgan, who lived in Hong Kong for twelve years, arrived in 1996 in the dying days of the British Empire.

The sheer density of the housing was hard to grasp and I thought it very odd that people would hang their washing out to dry on poles from tower block windows. It took me a long time to find my way around, but once I did, Hong Kong [got] under my skin and I wondered how I could live anywhere else.

Hong Kong may have looked entirely different back in 1937, but it still must have been a culture shock for Ciss. She had given up a suburban house and garden for a flat above a shop. Don and Ciss were expected (and could now afford) to employ local staff to cook, clean and babysit, yet Ciss's own sister, May, remained a domestic servant all her working life, even though she rose through the ranks to become a cook/housekeeper.

As Ciss no longer had to look after a home, she wasted no time in going out to work.

Molly took some time to adjust to their new life, too. She didn't like the first school she was sent to, the all-girls Assunta Convent, finding the atmosphere far too studious. All her Chinese and Indian classmates took their school work very seriously, even at age eleven. Molly recalls going home with a new Chinese friend and all the girl wanted to do was get out her books and swot. This didn't suit Molly at all – she was high-spirited and liked larking about.

It didn't take her long to find the other expat children,

who seemed to be having fun at their school while she was stuck in a boring convent. Molly told her parents she was unhappy and wanted to join her friends at CBS (Central British School). She had learned from an early age that the secret to getting her own way was to play one parent off against the other and ask her father first, which infuriated Ciss.

CBS had around 300 pupils, and although it was co-educational, it was for Europeans only, apart from one or two Chinese children whose families were wealthy and influential. Perhaps because she was still only young and final exams were still a long way off, Molly's recollections of CBS read like those of a wild-child at St Trinian's. Her Convent school in England had been strict, and Deal had been a quiet seaside backwater where everyone knew everybody else, but now here she was at a fee-paying school, making friends with expatriate children from around the world.

At CBS, Molly relished her new-found freedom. She recalled being told off for talking too much, and often being sent out of the French class by the teacher, Madame Tazarty. This would have been no surprise to Ciss, as Molly had turned into a chatterbox at home. Madame Tazarty owned a Chinese junk which was moored in Hong Kong harbour and used for parties, and Molly had plenty to say about her bohemian dress sense, which caused much amusement amongst the girls. She appeared to find her clothes in second-hand shops and would turn up to school wearing the oddest combination of outfits: one day dressed in a figure-hugging Chinese cheongsam dress, the next in a circular gypsy skirt teamed with a pair of trousers.

Another reason why Molly loved Hong Kong so much was because Ciss now went out to work so she could do as she liked after school. And for the first time in her life, she had a boyfriend. Molly met Igor, a Russian unlike any of the other boys she'd ever met. They used to hold hands at the cinema, perhaps the one in Nathan Road that Joyce Fitch describes.

Igor had an air of mystery about him. According to a family friend, Igor's grandfather had been an Admiral in the Russian Imperial Navy and the family had ended up in Hong Kong because they were White Russians, fleeing from communism. They brought with them a grandmother, referred to as *Babushka*, who spoke no more than a few words of English. Molly often wondered what became of Igor and his family, in particular whether they got out of Hong Kong before the Japanese occupation in 1941.

When they weren't out at the cinema with their various boyfriends, the girls would hang out together and have fun. Molly loved company, took part in team sports and was an enthusiastic member of the Hong Kong Guides. Her closest friend in Hong Kong was Yseult Cooper, with whom she had been friends back in Kent. Yseult, according to Molly, never seemed to do any homework or revision but always came top of the class, whereas Molly languished at the bottom in almost every subject except English and History.

Joyce Fitch was also at CBS and remembers that it was well away from central Kowloon. She recalls catching the school bus in Nathan Road and being driven up a long steep hill for some miles until they arrived at a Chinese village. From there it was a walk through the paddy field to school.

The school closed in 1940 and became a military hospital used by the British, then after the invasion of Hong Kong at the end of 1941 it was occupied by the Japanese during the war years. In 1946, it reopened for business, and in 1948 it was renamed the King George V School. It is still regarded as one of Hong Kong's most prestigious schools; the sun may have well and truly set on the Empire, but one or two aspects of its legacy still remain.

In 1997, sixty years after my family arrived to live in

Hong Kong, former resident Rona had (quite literally) a bird's eye view of its handover ceremony as she flew over proceedings.

The pilot took off from Kai Tak (the old airport) and flew straight down the middle of Victoria Harbour. I was lucky enough to be on the right side of the plane to get a great view of the royal yacht, Britannia, which was waiting to whisk Governor Chris Patton away after the ceremony. It was a very moving moment in the last moments of colonial Hong Kong.

On weekends the Lamberts, along with the other FECB expat families, would travel together to their favourite beach, where they shared a beach hut, known as a matshed, with family friends. It was called 11½ Mile Beach (now called Lido Beach) as it was at the eleven and a half milestone on Castle Peak Road, New Territories.

(Figure 3.1 Molly being pushed up the peak can be viewed in the gallery section of the website: http://www.lambertnagle.com)

The extraordinary photo of Molly being carried in a sedan chair up the Peak is a stark reminder of the terrible inequality between the European ruling class and the local Chinese people. It must have been backbreaking work for the poor workers, but life was good for the young Europeans. When their parents were at work, or out for the evening, Molly and her friends would get up to no end of mischief. As soon as the coast was clear they nipped round to each other's houses, raiding the drinks cabinet and the box where the cigarettes were kept. Trying all the spirits, they then topped up the bottle with water in the hope that the parents wouldn't notice.

One friend's mother had a fantastic collection of evening dresses and jewellery, and this was a favourite house for the wayward girls. Rifling through her wardrobe, they tried on all the lovely clothes and accessorised them with matching jewellery. On one occasion, they were nearly caught as the parents came home earlier than expected. Egged on by Yseult, one of their other favourite pranks was to ring up any number in the phone book and pretend that they were swearing in Cantonese. However, whenever there was a parent in the house to keep an eye on them, the children would dutifully play endless games of Monopoly.

One of their other little games was to catch the ferry over to Hong Kong and purchase several stink bombs at Sincere's, a large department store in Central. On the way back home to Kowloon, the unruly children would throw the stink bombs down onto the poor unfortunate passengers on the lower deck. When they were at Molly's home, the girls would help 'water' the pot plants. As the Nathan Road flat was on the top floor, if they 'spilled' the water over the top of the verandah, the poor unsuspecting pedestrians below would get a soaking.

In those days, there were no air conditioners and the summers were so hot that my parents and I had special 'summer beds' (camp stretchers really). Also, I remember when it was very hot having to sleep under a mosquito net and being terrified of the horrible flying cockroaches. Amah sat beside my bed swatting with one of her clogs and I was almost too [petrified] to sleep.

(Molly's unpublished memoir.)

By 1939, the Sino-Japanese war was creeping ever closer as Japan made strategic gains in the New Territories, the area of China next to Hong Kong. And in the UK there was a real threat of war with Germany. In London, the Admiralty took the decision to relocate the FECB surveillance operation to Singapore. If it came to a showdown, Hong Kong would be unable to defend herself, while the new Singapore Naval Base had been designed to withstand any attack.

When the Lamberts were told they were being evacuated, they were sad to leave.

> *We left Hong Kong on an armed merchant cruiser, HMS Devonshire, and whilst en-route to Singapore we heard on the wireless that England [Britain] had declared war against Germany. It was an eerie feeling, and although I was only thirteen years old at the time, I was a little bit scared, although excited. I can remember that we were advised to carry our life-jackets around with us at all times and that there were one or two submarines on our tail.*

(Molly's unpublished memoir.)

The Lamberts were in a military convoy, and thus a legitimate target. As well as the naval personnel and their families, the ship was carrying the entire Hong Kong FECB surveillance operation, including all its cumbersome machinery and equipment. On the same day that war was declared, 3 September 1939, a German U-boat attacked a British civilian passenger ship off the coast of Ireland, the SS *Athenia* carrying 1400 passengers and crew. This was the first British ship to be torpedoed in the conflict with Germany, with the loss of 117 lives, and it must have been very unnerving hearing this news over the wireless while at sea. No doubt the families on board *Devonshire* were mightily relieved when they arrived in Singapore without incident.

CHAPTER 4
– FORTRESS SINGAPORE

Once in Singapore we were sent to the Singapore Naval Base where we had a house just overlooking a large dry dock.

(Molly's unpublished memoir.)

Molly had spent her early years living close to a naval dockyard, so wasn't fazed by her new home, but she had never seen anything on the scale of the base at Sembawang. At the tip of Singapore island, it faced the narrow strip of water towards mainland Malaya. It was a vast complex of some 21 square miles, and the dry dock, which Molly mentions, used for ship refitting and repair, was the largest in the world. The base had a workforce numbering in the thousands, driving the giant cranes, fastening the rivets and engineering the machine tools. And then there were all the other staff – cleaners to clerks to Commander-in-Chief. It even had its own police force.

As well as the HQ of the British strategic defence of Malaya and her allies, the naval base was a Royal Navy shore station. Like any other military installation, media reports of day-to-day activities were forbidden. But when it suited them, the British government was keen to get the message across to would-be aggressors not to mess with Britannia. The continuing supply of Malaya's natural resources, tin and rubber, were vital if the Allies were going to stand any chance of winning the war. The official propaganda photographs published in 1940 boasted the might of Singapore's seemingly impregnable naval defences, the claim being that Singapore could withstand any attack. But what the British government failed to mention was that it couldn't afford to give the new and shiny naval base its own naval fleet as all of its ships were needed for the war in Europe.

As well as strict controls on reporting, disciplinary offences were taken very seriously. When a police constable with the naval base police fell asleep on duty and then went absent without leave for three days, he was prosecuted. He was, he told the court, fed up with his living conditions: an attap (palm) hut in the middle of a swamp. When he couldn't face going to work, he decided on the spur of the moment to head off into town. To a civilian, going AWOL and falling asleep on duty might seem trivial, but the policeman was convicted and sentenced to either a fine of $100/£12 (equivalent to £500 today) for each crime or three weeks 'vigorous imprisonment' –hard labour, toiling in hot conditions in construction or road building.

If others had grumbles about living conditions, they were wise enough not to go public. If you joined the services, in exchange for a secure job you had to be prepared to sign away your individual rights for the greater good. And no one knew this more than Don Lambert.

Home life for the Lamberts was vastly more comfortable than that of the hapless policeman. Surrounded by dozens of other identical houses, bungalow No 3, or 'The Corner House', was a mock-Tudor style house on stilts with wooden shutters. Concrete steps led up to the front door. There was a spacious covered terrace enclosed by a balcony open to the elements, which was closed off in bad weather by outdoor blinds. It was furnished with two roomy armchairs and a rosewood occasional table on top of which sat an ornate Chinese lamp. To one side was a bamboo dining table.

Compared with their small flat above the shop in Hong Kong, The Corner House was positively luxurious. And best of all, it had a fenced back garden with a lawn and two flower beds planted with red canna lilies, palm trees and, rather incongruously, an English style hedge. It was big enough not only for Molly to have a swing, but to have another pet as she still missed her fox terrier. It wasn't long before the family got themselves a cat and a poodle called Fifi.

The naval base was self-contained and had churches, cinemas, a hospital and sports facilities with playing fields. The downside was that it was 16 miles from Singapore town. And thirteen-year-old Molly found herself marooned. As her mother never found the confidence to get behind the wheel of a car, if Molly wanted to go anywhere, her father had to drive her.

All that changed when Steve came into their lives. Norman Stephens, known to everyone as Steve, was Don's colleague. At twenty-eight, he had the air of someone older than his years. Always smartly turned out, he was seldom seen without his pipe or cigar. With his dry wit and fogey-ish manner, he was an amusing companion.

He and Molly seemed to get along famously. They went on outings to Singapore, the cinema, to tea, as well as on adventures in his little Riley, which had been christened the Jitterbug.

One of Molly and Steve's favourite little jaunts was to Alkaff Lake Gardens. The gardens were situated between the naval base and Singapore town in a well-to-do neighbourhood of large houses and leafy streets. Molly loved the ten acres of Japanese style water gardens as she could run across the bridges, play under the arches and even take tea with Steve in a tea house, but it must have taken a bit of persuasion to get Steve to hire one of the little row boats as he wasn't exactly the outdoors sort. Taking in a play at the open-air stage was more to his taste.

Molly was glad of the distraction of her little trips with Steve, as she hadn't yet had the chance to meet new friends her own age.

Schooling for me and the other three families in our group was a problem and we had a year being taught privately by an extremely good teacher who inspired me to work harder at my studies, and try to get a good pass when the time came for me to take School Certificate.

In the family album is a photo of a very smartly dressed young woman in a skirt suit with hat, heels and clutch bag. Molly has captioned the photo 'Miss Langford' rather than using a Christian name, which leads me to believe this was her teacher.

It surprised me that the Lamberts were struggling to find the right school, as Singapore by then had a population of one million. Part of British-ruled Malaya, the little island at the southern end of the Malay peninsula was a prized possession of the Empire. A port city, lying on the equator, it was not only the gateway to South East Asia, but strategically placed, roughly halfway between the UK and her allies, Australia and New Zealand.

After three months living in Singapore, in December 1939 the Lambert family celebrated their first tropical Christmas. They had friends around for drinks before decamping to Singapore Swimming Club for lunch. The swimming club was housed in a magnificent art deco building which at that time overlooked the beach at Tanjong Rhu. (Land reclamation projects have since meant that the club has lost its prime waterfront location and is now some way from the sea.) Set up in 1894 for European men only, it wasn't until 1931 that women were permitted, and it took another twenty years before they allowed Asian members. Admiralty staff may have been given a discount, as Don and Ciss, and their colleagues, wouldn't have been able to afford the membership fees otherwise.

Molly and her father loved the outdoor lifestyle of Singapore and took advantage of it at every opportunity. A keen tennis player, Molly regularly partnered Don in doubles matches. Nimble around a tennis court, she would play close to the net, and even in her late fifties could still thrash me in a game. As well as having a passion for tennis, Don was a keen golfer, but Molly didn't have the patience or the precision for golf. Ciss had no interest in sports, but started to enjoy swimming in the sea once the family moved to the Far East.

As well as sports, Molly loved dancing, yet another interest she shared with her father.

Figure 4.1 New Year's Eve 1940 (Back row R to L Don Lambert, Middle Row R to L, Ciss Lambert, Front Row R to L, Norman Stephens (Steve), Molly Lambert

By mid-September 1940, the family had been in Singapore for a year. Molly was fourteen-and-a-half, an awkward age for any teenager. She was, at times, introspective and dreamy, a trait she inherited from her mother, who was quiet and shy until you got to know her. But for the rest of the time she was a chatterbox, and that drove her mother to distraction.

I remember Ciss, or Nan as we knew her, would remark in her soft Cork lilt that "Molly had been vaccinated with a gramophone needle".

She got this side of her personality from her father: Don loved socialising and was always inviting friends home for meals and impromptu get-togethers, usually forgetting to tell Ciss.

Molly's schooling had been disrupted because of the evacuation from Hong Kong, but under the tutelage of her private teacher, she was now studying hard. In a year's time, she would be sitting her School Certificate, which she needed to pass to get a decent job. But the biggest question for the family in late 1940 was at which school Molly would sit these exams.

My parents had heard of a very good school (a convent) in a cool hill-station named Cameron Highlands, and after much discussion and persuasion on my part, they reluctantly agreed to send me there. I was in seventh heaven because at last I was going to a 'real' boarding school, where it would also be cool.

Don and Ciss were hesitant about sending Molly to school in a remote jungle region, 300 miles away. Travelling there was an adventure in itself as it meant taking the Night Mail Train to Kuala Lumpur, and then changing trains for Tapah Road. The final stage of the journey was an hour-and-a-half's drive up the treacherous hairpin bends to the Highlands. If relations with Japan deteriorated any further and the school was required to evacuate, it wouldn't be easy to get Molly out of Cameron Highlands in a hurry. Then there were the school fees, uniform and travel expenses to consider. But Molly kept on at her parents, enthusing about the reputation of the school and the importance of a good school in her School Certificate year.

By Christmas 1940, Don and Ciss had reluctantly decided to give in to Molly's demands. The apple of her father's eye, Molly knew that if she could talk him round,

Ciss would go along with his decision, even if privately she didn't agree. Ciss thought that Don spoilt Molly and gave in too easily, although she never criticised him to his face. Realising that at last she would now have the chance to make new friends, for Christmas Don and Ciss gave Molly an autograph book. Her sweet tribute to her friends is touching, but the line that moves me most is the hope that she would live to see old age.

To all my friends
Go little book, go far and near,
To all my friends I love so dear,
And urge them all to write a page,
To comfort me in my old age.
With love from Molly. Xmas 1940.
(Inscription in Molly's autograph book.)

Molly had by now lived in the Far East for three years. What a world away it was from the ordinary life she'd left behind in seaside England.

CHAPTER 5
– IN THE SHADOW OF WAR

In February 1941 at the age of fourteen, Molly finally got her wish. Full of excitement, she left Singapore for her new school, hundreds of miles away upcountry in Malaya. Her notion of what boarding school was like had been shaped by the escapades of the teenage heroines in Angela Brazil's novels, but the reality was rather different. Molly, who had always hated early mornings, was no longer allowed to sleep in, and had to get up with everyone else. And every hour of her day was timetabled. There were school lessons and team games, and on weekends, church services.

This was the first time Molly had ever stayed away from home overnight, and when she first got there, she cried often. She missed being the centre of attention and playing with her pets. She missed her friend Yseult, her parents and her outings with Steve in his little car. But as she had lobbied so hard to go to this particular school, she had little choice but to stick it out. To cheer her up, Steve wrote to her, entertaining her with gossip and stories of mutual acquaintances back in Singapore.

Once she'd got over that initial bout of homesickness, Molly began to flourish. She loved that the Highlands, some 5,900 feet above sea level, were cool, sometimes even cold, as the temperature never got above 75 degrees Fahrenheit. And it was the perfect climate for team games.

We had some interesting games of hockey: one nun in

particular used to join in, and as their habits were rather voluminous, we sometimes lost sight of the ball, then discovered it in the lap of Madame St Mary Michael.

After a vigorous game of hockey, the girls had worked up quite an appetite.

Because the Pensionnat Notre Dame was a French order, most of the nuns were French, Irish or English, but the lay sisters – recruited from local areas – were taught to cook in the French way. To this day, I remember the rice puddings, strawberries (which they grew themselves), fresh rolls (being prodded in the back for slouching and told to "Break your rolls, girls"). On special Feast Days and Holidays of Obligation, we were allowed special fizzy drinks (Fraser & Neave), potato chips and delicious desserts.

Being an only child, I thrived in this environment.

Molly found it lonely at times being an 'only'. She said she would have loved a brother or a sister, but what she hadn't considered was that she'd have had to compete with a sibling for her father's attention.

It must have been quiet back home at No 3 bungalow without Molly's constant chatter and Don, in particular would have missed her. When Don and Ciss did have time off, I'm sure they would have relished a trip up to the Highlands to visit her. A favourite hill-station for European expats, it was the perfect place to escape the oppressive heat and humidity. Surrounded by mountains, the Highlands reminded visitors of the climate and the familiar scenery of the countries they'd left behind, half a world away. Expats were so taken with the place that they began to build little mock Tudor style bungalows up at the hill-station for their retirement.

By 1941, the war in Europe was in its second year, and while the conflict for Molly might have seemed very far away, it wasn't for her fellow pupils.

My classmates comprised the daughters of planters, tin miners, government officials and diplomats. At that time when the Blitz in the UK was really bad, many families of rubber planters, civil services and medical services decided to bring their sons and daughters out to Malaya where they thought they would be safer.

Less than a year later, those same children would find themselves caught up in a global conflict of a magnitude the world had never seen before.

At long last I started to realise that I really had to work hard at every subject in order to get School Certificate, which meant in those days that I could get a better job with prospects, and I'd not have to go to work in a factory or serve in Woolworths!

Surrounded by her boarding school classmates, all of whom were studying hard for their exams, Molly was, for the first time in her life, motivated to succeed academically. She'd left it rather late, but made up for lost time by revising hard in the holidays.

As we were all backward in Latin, we of the Seventh Form (nine girls in all) received special lessons from the wife of the District Officer in Tanah Rata. I learned to ride, play the piano and work. I became so studious that I brought a suitcase full of books to study during the holidays, and eventually became the school 'swot'.

Being Catholic, I went through all the devotions and did a lot of praying (especially before exams), and even considered becoming a nun myself at some stage.

Eventually, the dreaded day came – when we of the Seventh Form had to sit the School Certificate exam. We had all been well prepared and tutored, and now the moment of truth was at hand. I'm sure exams were easier in those days, or perhaps I had really studied all nine subjects that I had taken and was blessed with a photographic memory, as I had no trouble in answering the papers – even in Latin unseen translations!

(Molly's memoirs 1988)

Molly wrote these words nearly fifty years later when she was sixty-two. It's understandable that she looked back on her time there with such nostalgia, but just when she was finally settling in and starting to stretch herself academically, world events took a dramatic turn.

One reason Don and Ciss had been against sending Molly to school so far away was that they spent their working lives listening to and intercepting messages sent by the Japanese naval fleet. Privy to this classified intelligence, they were convinced that a war with Japan was inevitable. In December 1941, just as Molly was sitting School Certificate, the schoolgirls heard some ominous news on the radio:

We were all greatly encouraged when we heard of the arrival of the mighty battleship, Prince of Wales and cruiser Repulse and all thought they would soon 'sort out' the Japanese. Then we heard on the news that the Japanese had attacked Pearl Harbour on December 2nd, 1941, thus drawing the Americans into the conflict – to be followed by air raids on Singapore. Most of the children not taking School Certificate had been sent back to their homes.

December 2 was, in fact, the date that *Prince of Wales* and *Repulse* arrived at the Singapore Naval Base with great fanfare. The attack on Pearl Harbour took place on 7 December, 8 December in Malaya, at the same time as the first Japanese bombing raid on Singapore. It was 4am in Singapore when Don and Ciss were woken by the air raid sirens. Their worst fears had come to pass. Their darling Molly was hundreds of miles away. All they could do was pray she would get home safely, but as a former Royal Marine, Don would have known only too well what perfect cover a remote jungle region could provide for an advancing Japanese land invasion.

There were four of us Seventh Formers left – two girls whose families were in the diplomatic service in Bangkok (they spent the whole of the war years in the Cameron Highlands and I think their parents went to a Japanese POW camp). One girl

[Marjorie] and I, both from Singapore and scheduled to take one more examination, were left. Neither of us realised the seriousness of what was happening. The Japanese were advancing rapidly down the Malay Peninsula, thus cutting off the Cameron Highlands and another hill-station.

Marjorie and I travelled down 'The Hill' for the last time together, then boarded the train at Tapah [for] Kuala Lumpur.

I made that same trip fifty years later in a modern car with power steering. It took over an hour and a half to negotiate the hairpin bends on that treacherous road. In 1941 it was little more than a dirt track.

We were to board the Night Mail Train from KL to Singapore where our parents would be waiting for us. We had dinner with one of our friends in KL and their cook-boy and driver took us to KL station. Suddenly the air raid sirens sounded – the cookie hurriedly took us to the subway under the station.

We were two rather frightened schoolgirls in our grey and blue school uniforms and hats, and suddenly we found ourselves in a crowded subway, crammed with soldiers from all sorts of different regiments on the way up the Peninsula to fight the Japanese. The soldiers comforted us with sweets and cigarettes (we didn't smoke) and made jokes. It was a relief to hear the 'All-Clear' sounding, but I shall always remember those brave men, and wonder to this day how many survived.

It was an eleven to twelve hour journey from KL to Singapore and I doubt if the two girls got much sleep that night.

We boarded the train again and arrived in Singapore where our anxious parents were awaiting us at the station. The war had come to our doorstep at last.

As Molly heard about Pearl Harbour up at school, she and Marjorie must have caught the train to Kuala Lumpur on the following day, 9 December. That would have meant they arrived in Singapore on 10 December. Molly and Marjorie were very relieved to be home, but their euphoria was short-lived as that same day tragedy struck the naval base. Molly describes how she heard the news that the pride of the British naval fleet, *Prince of Wales* and *Repulse*, had been bombed and sunk.

I remember my father's ashen face when coming up the steps of our bungalow as he announced that both these mighty ships had been sunk off Kelantan and nearly all hands had perished off the Malayan coast. Our naval padre, a Father Cunningham who used often to visit us for drinks and chats, went at once to help the few survivors.

The two ships sank at around 1pm on 10 December and survivors were being pulled from the sea throughout the night. Out of a total crew of 2,900, 840 men had either been killed in the bombing or drowned in the aftermath. It was the Royal Navy's greatest loss of life in any one incident.

The next few weeks we spent going down to the air raid shelters on the naval base. My father got very cross with me when I wanted to go outside to look at the sky and our amah was scared out of her wits. No one, as historians of those times have reiterated, really treated the Japanese seriously.

No one, that is, apart from Molly's father. Since the start of the war with Germany, he had joined the Royal Navy Volunteer Reserve and knew very well that the entire naval fleet had been commandeered for the war effort. And if Singapore was attacked from the sea, there was no replacement battleship or spare cruiser that could come to their rescue. The news media upheld the official line, which was that Singapore would easily see off the Japanese threat, but it was just a ploy to boost public morale, at least among the civilian population.

Don and Ciss hid their misgivings from Molly, and kept up the pretence as they were swept up in the social whirl of Christmas and New Year preparations. Molly did hear them talking late into the night, although she didn't know what was troubling them.

The residents were still going to dances and cocktail parties, hoping against hope that Singapore was still impregnable, and would not fall to the Japanese as Hong Kong had done.

The British administration in Hong Kong had surrendered to the Japanese on Christmas Day 1941. News had filtered out of atrocities committed during the Japanese invasion. At one hospital, all the wounded soldiers were murdered and a group of civilian nurses gang raped.

All eyes now were on Singapore. Behind the scenes, the Admiralty quietly began to make arrangements to evacuate the naval base. They kept their plans a carefully guarded secret.

As the air raids increased and the Japanese advanced towards Singapore, my father tried to persuade my mother to leave, with other evacuees, and go down to Australia. This she flatly refused to do, and I was in agreement – we three would stick together whatever happened. My father was more realistic than we were as he hinted darkly at keeping two bullets, one for my mother and one for me, rather than have us fall into Japanese hands.

A few people were leaving in dribs and drabs, and the navy was (it was rumoured) preparing to evacuate to Darwin. Plans then changed and we received the news that we were to prepare to be evacuated to an unknown destination. My memories are rather vague at this point, but afterwards I learned that my father had taken our dog to be 'put down'. Our car was jettisoned, and all the alcohol in the house washed down the nearest sink.

Singapore was awash with abandoned cars, many of them still with their keys left in them. By January 1941 you couldn't even give one away. In February 1942, as the Japanese invasion began, many of these abandoned vehicles were deliberately driven into the harbour to prevent the Japanese from landing their ships.

My mother managed to salvage a Balinese head, a barrel load of china and a camphor wood chest. We were luckier than most: we got away with a few possessions and the clothes we stood up in.

The official announcement of the departure of the Commander-in-Chief was made on the front page of the Straits Times on 8 January 1942, the day *after* the first convoy left. It stated: Vice-Admiral Sir Geoffrey Layton, Commander-in-Chief Eastern Fleet, has left Singapore 'to organise the Eastern Fleet so that the Allies can gain sea supremacy as soon as possible'. No mention was made of the destination of this convoy, nor that almost the entire spying operation and staff were on board, as officially the FECB didn't even exist.

The convoy of Royal Navy ships sailing out of the Singapore Naval Base must have been a terrifying sight for the remaining residents, especially local Chinese who had nowhere to flee and whose own homeland was now in Japanese hands. They'd been led to believe that the British would protect them, but in the last chaotic days before Singapore fell, it was every man for himself. The furniture, clothes, car and other possessions the Lamberts had to leave behind could be replaced, but they were heartbroken to have to say their goodbyes to the Chinese family who worked for them.

I don't remember what happened to our very loyal cook-boy, his wife and several children – I hope they survived to serve their Japanese masters. It was not until several years later that we learned that our house had received a direct hit.

I don't know the names of my grandparents' cook and his wife, but I have included their photograph in the hope that somebody might recognise them. I can only hope that those little boys grew up to be fathers and even grandfathers.

(Figure 5.1 The Lamberts Cook and His Family, Singapore Naval Base can be viewed in the gallery section of the website: http://www.lambertnagle.com)

We went wherever directed. All naval personnel were sent off in a convoy and our eventual destination was Colombo where a new naval headquarters was set up.

A skeleton staff, including Steve, stayed behind in Singapore to shred all remaining paperwork so that not a single scrap of evidence of the code breaking operation was left for the invading Japanese. The last British naval convoy bound for Colombo left Singapore at the end of January 1942. For the remaining civilians left behind, there was a desperate scramble for passage on any available vessel, seagoing or not, willing to take them.

On 15 February, British forces in Singapore surrendered. Singapore was a fortress no more.

CHAPTER 6
– ESCAPE FROM COLOMBO

Molly was sad to wave Singapore goodbye as it became an ever smaller dot on the horizon. She felt a mixture of curiosity and fear about where they were heading next.

On their way out to Hong Kong in 1937, the Lamberts had stopped off at Ceylon (Sri Lanka), the island off the southern coast of India. But this time round their experience didn't seem quite so pleasant. Writing in 1988, Molly recalls what happened when they first arrived.

We were told we would be billeted at what sounded a fairly decent hotel – how dumb we were. I shall never forget arriving at the hotel only to walk over two drunken matelots being violently sick on the threshold. Both my mother and I were horrified, and my poor father was confronted with two weeping women. Mama and I just couldn't cope with the situation. The 'hotel' was little more than a sleazy boarding house – where sailors on shore leave slept off their drunken antics. It was most unsuitable for families with children.

My father had been desperately searching for other accommodation, and he had the good fortune to meet 'Robbie' Robertson and his wife Susie, who took pity on us and took us in as lodgers at their home in Bambalapitiya, just outside Colombo on the way to Mount Lavinia. Robbie was manager of the wines and spirits department at Cargills, Colombo, and Susie was in charge of ladies' lingerie. They were so good to us; we can never repay them.

Eventually, on one of the last ships to leave Singapore, a very dear friend of the family, namely Mr N.D.E Stephens, Civil Engineer [family friend Steve], and Judy, a shorthand typist, arrived, and they too joined the little evacuated family.

Bambalapitiya, right next to the sea, was a very tropical and romantic place to stay. With the waves breaking on the shore, it was a real haven to us. I can't remember a great deal now, but once, walking by myself on the sea-shore, I saw a familiar face. It was Vice-Admiral Sir Geoffrey Leyton, whom my father and I had partnered in a tennis match what seemed aeons ago. I don't know whether he recognised me, but I can remember asking him whether we would win the war. He was very nice to a young, impressionable fifteen-year-old, and whatever he said to me then, I was encouraged. I only felt frustrated that I was still too young to join any of the armed forces and do my duty for my country. My father and mother were still working for naval intelligence, and I was trying to keep up my school work and music.

Ciss and many of the other wives of the codes and cipher clerks were employed by the Admiralty as local staff, but their contribution to the war effort was never formally acknowledged as their names don't appear in any official records. While Ciss and Don went to work, Molly did her best to study. Still only fifteen, there was a slim chance that she could manage to get into senior school and university. Her School Certificate exam papers had been sent back to England for marking, but now that Malaya was under occupation, there was nowhere to send the results. Three months into what should have been their university entrance year, none of the students knew if they had passed or failed.

By early April 1942, the family had been in Ceylon for three months, and they took the opportunity to spend the Easter weekend upcountry with friends who owned a tea estate. They then returned to Colombo to some very grave news.

Our train was delayed for a very long time, and it was only when we got back to our billets that we learned the Japanese had attacked Colombo with dire results, there being very little air cover from the British pilots. Things were chaotic. All the staff of the local hotel were hotfooting it out of Colombo as fast as they could, and things were definitely not looking good for the Eastern Fleet. At this stage, and probably as any other [parent] would have done, my [father] arranged for my mother and I to return to the UK.

(Extract from Molly's unpublished memoir.)

At the quayside, Don handed Molly the green log book where he had recorded their voyage out to Hong Kong back in 1937. He told Molly that he wanted to read about her adventures, but really it was a way of keeping her busy so that she wouldn't fret over their enforced separation.

April 21st 1942

Left Melbourne Ave at about 7.30 and arrived at jetty at 8am. People on board *Devonshire* left first and we left at 8.45 after saying goodbye to Daddy and Steve.

Sailed at 1.00 and thought of Daddy and everyone as we watched Colombo disappear from view. Made friends with Dene Beaver and we had a nice afternoon talking about old Hong Kong days. Also met David Albrect who is an old CBS [Central British School] boy. This is a lovely ship – much nicer than the *Devonshire*, which is in this convoy. There are three big ships, three small ones and two escorts, so we should be OK. All the boys [staff] on this ship are Chinese and wear long coats like they used to in Hong Kong. We should be out of the danger zone by tomorrow, which will be a bit of a relief.

(Source: Don & Molly Lambert's logbook – original held in Department of Documents, Imperial War Museum, London)

Molly and Ciss were in the convoy MB2 (Colombo to Bombay). The three big ships included *Devonshire* and *Shengking* and the two escorts were HMS *Falmouth* and HMS *Lismore*.

April 22nd

Quite an uneventful day–the ship has been rolling a bit and some people are feeling a bit sea-sick. We have been hugging the coast all day, and one or two planes came over this afternoon. [Likely to be Japanese aircraft observing the size and speed of the convoy.] We tried to see the people on the *Devonshire* with a pair of binoculars, but couldn't distinguish anyone very clearly. Rather boring on this ship – nothing much to do.

April 23rd

Nothing much happened. We left the convoy at 8 in the morning off Kuchin in South India, about 150 miles up the coast. [Once an unarmed ship left a convoy it was vulnerable to attack from enemy submarines even if it was carrying civilian passengers.]

Three days into her voyage, Molly wrote to family friend Steve. They had been lodging at the same house in Colombo and had begun spending more time together.

A ship
Somewhere at sea
24th April 1942

My dear Steve,

It is three days since we left Colombo and at last I am writing to you. I would have done so before, only there was no ink or paper to be found anywhere on this ship, and I had to beg, borrow or steal what I am using now.

It is hard to believe that we have been gone only three days, because to me it seems like three years. We left the jetty about five minutes after you said goodbye, so the agony wasn't prolonged too much, thank goodness. It was quite bad enough, though, waving goodbye to Daddy until he was just a speck in the distance, and Mummy and I felt... just a bit fed up. We didn't sail until about 1 [pm], so we had to hang around until then, doing nothing. The ship is quite a decent one and can go quite fast, which is rather a blessing. Up to now, everything has been alright, so we have been quite lucky (I hope, I hope).

[All letters were censored for security purposes in wartime in case they fell into enemy hands. What Molly wants to say, but can't, is that because the ship is fast, they've been able to outrun any enemy submarines that may have been on their tail.]

Mummy and I were pretty unlucky over the tables in the dining room, because we have a pretty awful bunch at our table. There is one woman who sits next to me who absolutely puts me off all my food. She is simply ghastly! Ugh! I'm afraid I'm rather rude, but I just can't look at her, never mind talk to her. You remember that girl in slacks whom you pointed out to me on the jetty? Well, she and her mother sit opposite Mummy and I and they never say a word. Then there is Mrs Wright, who criticises every dish that comes up and tells us there are caterpillars in the cabbage, etc., etc. So altogether I haven't felt much like eating at all since we came on board, although I still don't do too badly.

Mummy and I were lucky enough to get a cabin to ourselves on this ship, but I doubt whether we will be so lucky on the next.

[She goes on to say that she and Ciss are so grateful not to be sharing with any of their horrible dining companions.]

I have written to Daddy today as well, and I hope to

post both letters tomorrow when we arrive at our first port of call. [*Molly wasn't permitted to mention the port by name.*] I hope we pick Judy up there, because she only went a week before us and it's quite likely that she has had to wait there. [*Judy was a shorthand typist for the Admiralty who had been billeted in the same house in Colombo.*] I think I will wait before posting this letter and then I'll be able to tell you.

Funnily enough, there is an old CBS [*Central British School*] boy on this ship too. He is in the Air Force and was in Singapore while we were there. His name is David Albrect and he is quite nice. I showed him some CBS mags and he was quite thrilled, because he knew practically all the people in them. All he, Dene and I do is sit and talk about Hong Kong. There is only one deck game, and we can't play that all the time. The only other thing to do is walk, and there isn't very much deck space to do it in.

This morning Mummy had her fortune told by Mrs Simmonds, and she said that we weren't going to go right home, but would get off at some port and wait for Daddy there. I shan't mind that as long as it isn't Bombay. I want my fortune told too. I don't really believe in fortune-telling, but I am just a bit curious about the future. Gosh! A week today I shall be sweet sixteen and never been kissed. (Ahem! Can't say that now can I?) If she tells my fortune at tea-time today I'll tell you, if it's interesting.

[*Reading between the lines, the likeliest candidate for Molly's affections could only have been Steve.*]

How is the jolly old work going? Have you given dear Mr Wilson a dose of arsenic yet? I shan't be surprised to read of his murder in the papers one day and I don't suppose that you will be the only one that has had a hand in it. I would have done it myself if there had been time! I don't know him, of course, but I know he's working you to the bone, giving you prickly heat, worrying you, turning you into a Bolshevik and preventing you from going home, and that's quite good enough for me! I hope your letter made him sit up and think a bit, and I hope by the time this letter reaches you, that the situation will have improved a lot.

[*Molly seems to have forgotten that all letters sent to and from the FECB were being read by the official naval censor. Her little indiscretion of referring to Mr Wilson by name must have caused Steve some serious embarrassment.*]

I shouldn't worry too much about him, and above all, don't let him get you down. I suppose I don't know anything about it really, and maybe I'm talking through my hat, but it seems clear to me that it's he who is in the wrong, because you get on well with all the others. He is the only one out of six or seven whom you haven't got on with, so he must be at fault, not you. Anyway, don't, don't, don't let him turn you into someone with an embittered and cynical outlook on life, because it wouldn't be you, and we'd rather have you. This sounds a bit incoherent, but I think you understand what I'm trying to say. I'm like you. I can always write things much better than I can say them, and this is what I was trying to say on Monday night, but couldn't.

[*Monday was the night before Molly left and it seems to me that she and Steve must have been alone – perhaps walking together along the beach in Colombo. In her memoirs, she recalled the area as 'a very tropical and romantic place to stay'.*]

Well, to change the subject, the weather has been very good all during the trip, although it was a bit choppy on the first day, and quite a number of people felt bad. Of course I didn't, although I must admit I didn't feel much like eating anything at the first three meals. Mrs Simmonds only got up today. She's an awfully bad sailor and has been ill all the time.

It is tea-time now, so I must stop for the time being. I'm not going to finish this letter today because I want to wait and see what happens tomorrow, so I'll just say BBC closing down for the time being.

April 24th

We expect to arrive in Bombay tomorrow and have increased our speed a little. Spent quite an energetic evening playing deck quoits with David and another chap. Dene and I were shown over the wireless operations room and I collected the autographs of the ship's crew for a souvenir. Chief Engineer says we will arrive at about eight tomorrow. I hope we can go ashore, although it's a pretty filthy hole if I can remember rightly.

April 25th

Arrived Bombay but didn't go ashore. At three o'clock we were told that we were to go on board the *Aramika*, a big 42,000 ton ship which was supposed to be sailing at five, but then we were told that it was full up and we will have to wait for the next convoy. Everyone is very fed up and no one seems to know what is going to happen to us.

April 26th

Still anchored in Bombay harbour. We don't seem to be going ashore today either. It's awfully annoying being stuck out here, not knowing what is going to happen to us, and no one seems to bother what we do. Feel very fed up.

April 28th 1942

We went ashore today and saw the sights of Bombay. It is really a very pretty place, and very much cleaner than we expected. I think we must have seen the worst part of it when we passed through before. There are some lovely big shops and we bought quite a few things. We had a ride on one of the double-decker buses and had lunch and tea in a place called Monginis where they sell delicious ice cream, cold drinks and heavenly cakes. A very nice day.

April 29th

Didn't go ashore, but had quite a pleasant day on board. Heard we are disembarking tomorrow. Quite sorry.

April 30th

Got up early and packed once more and eventually a launch arrived to take us to the *Westernland*, a Dutch boat due to sail on May 1st. We were quite sorry to be leaving the *Shengking*.

The *Westernland* is a huge ship of about 23,000 tons, and as there are only about seventy-seven passengers in all aboard – there is tons of room. We have a cabin to ourselves, thank goodness, and as it is a four-berther, there is plenty of room.

The ship's officers are very nice indeed, and the food and accommodation are excellent. I think we will have quite a good time, only I wish there were more passengers. The only new passengers are a lot of naval officers and one woman with three little boys. We made friends with a Lieut. Parsons who escaped from Hong Kong. He is quite nice, and knows a lot of people that we used to know.

It is Princess Juliana's birthday today, and the crew and some of the passengers kicked up a bit of a row during the night.

May 1st 1942

It is my birthday today, but we couldn't celebrate it very much because we weren't allowed ashore. However I had a very pleasant surprise at lunch-time, because the Chief Steward found out about it and made me a cake with sixteen candles on it. The cake was delicious, and somehow or other there was enough for everybody, which was very nice.

We sailed at 1pm, and just as we were leaving, the appearance of a very large whale caused great excitement.

After lunch, the Chief Steward invited us to tea in his cabin. After that I watched some people playing shuffleboard. It looks quite difficult. Had quite good fun after dinner and sat in a bar for the first time. I only had a lime juice, so it was quite alright. Everyone drank my health and everything was quite jolly.

May 2nd

Nothing very much of note happened today. The ship does a lot of zig-zagging [to avoid detection by enemy U-boats] and does not seem to go very fast. Deck games have started, but only a few people play them. They aren't a very lively crowd.

[The next two days passed uneventfully. The sea was very calm and the weather perfect, although Molly found their stuffy cabin unbearably hot at night.]

May 5th

Today was Mrs Wright's birthday and she had a cake just like mine, except that it was made of wood! The Chief Steward gave her a real one afterwards, which was very nice. After dinner, the Chief Steward asked us to come down to his cabin for a drink, and we all drank Mrs Wright's health in white wine. It was jolly nice too. I had two glasses.

A ship
Somewhere at sea
7th May 1942

Dearest Stevie,

[*Molly begins by apologising for not having written sooner but she couldn't settle down to letter writing. She's frustrated that she has to leave out much of the information to appease the censor.*]

You probably know by now that we were unlucky enough to miss the big boat that we were supposed to go on owing to some silly ass at the Naval Office forgetting all about us. (I hope no one from the Naval Office reads this). We were very fed up about the whole business because we had been looking forward very much to seeing everybody and having a good time with them. Actually I was much more fed up than Mummy because I did want to see Judy and Mooky *[Muriel Squibb]* and all the other Singapore Naval Base-ites. I was looking forward to some fun with them. It was just sickening to think that they were all on the same boat and we were stuck in (I can't say the name of the place) [*It was, in fact, Bombay*] waiting goodness knows how long for the next ship. To make matters worse, the beastly ship stuck around in the harbour for about two days and anchored just a little way from us, and we had to watch her sail out amidst much weeping, wailing and gnashing of teeth. I'm afraid the Lambert Waterworks Company had a very busy weekend altogether, because their owner was just too fed up for words. We weren't even allowed ashore for three days, and that was bad enough in itself. Still, when we did get ashore we had a lovely day.

There are some lovely big shops there and we did quite a lot of shopping. The only thing we regret is that we didn't buy enough, because we thought we were going ashore the next day. I very nearly bought a pair of shorts and a pair of shoes which were very cheap, but as we were rather short of funds we decided against them and now we wish we hadn't. Instead of buying a new pair of shorts, I renovated my old navy blue ones and took them up in the middle, and now they look quite smart and don't hang down the way they used to. I don't know what I would have done without them on this ship, because I wear them every day with a different shirt. It has been much too hot for slacks, and as all my dresses are packed, the shorts have been an absolute boon to me. It's rather lucky they are navy blue, because they don't show the dirt. Mummy has been living in her slacks the whole time, but she finds them very hot.

This ship is a lovely big one and there is tons of deck space, thank goodness. There are only seventy-seven passengers on board, including about fifty of the sort of people you like very much (ahem!) *[naval officers]*. Catch on? I can't say any more, but I think you get me, being good at riddles. It's rather like those cryptic crosswords we, or rather you, used to do on Sunday afternoons. Do you still do them? There are only about *[twenty-five]* women and children on board, and only four girls, including myself. The other three girls are the two Simmonds and that girl you pointed out on the jetty, the one wearing slacks. Altogether we are not exactly a very lively crowd on this boat. The two Simmonds get a good time, but they are older than me and I can't do the things they do. In any case, I don't want to. Sometimes I wish I was either older or younger, because sixteen is a terribly awkward age. You're too old to play with the kids (although I play with them sometimes) and too young to be grown-up, and you're just stuck between the two. It's horrid. I wouldn't mind at all if there was someone else to mess around with, but there isn't, unfortunately. Still, I have quite good fun really.

I have been doing quite a bit of shorthand and have been promised a typewriter. There are two lovely pianos on board and I spend every afternoon practising on the one in the dining saloon where no one can hear me. I get quite a lot of exercise in the evenings as well, playing deck games and dancing after dinner (at least, I danced last night). There are some twins on this ship and they are quite good dancers. One of them dances every night with Betty Simmonds, but the other one always plays chess (except last night). I am making myself a frock, so you see, I am not idle by any means. In fact, I haven't been bored once on this ship.

[*Molly tells Steve about what happened on her birthday and how embarrassed she felt at the attention.*] While we were having lunch we suddenly saw the Chief Steward bring in a huge cake with sixteen candles on it. Before I had time to wonder how on earth he knew it was my birthday, Mrs Simmonds went over to the piano and started playing 'Happy birthday to you', and everyone began singing it. Gosh! Was my face red! I thought I would sink through the floor! Still, it was terribly decent of the Chief Steward to go to all the trouble of making the cake and getting the right number of candles on it, but it still is a mystery to me how he knew.

Anyway, it was a very nice surprise and I certainly appreciated it. It was a lovely cake too, all decorated with big marzipan flowers. It was really a pity to cut it. Luckily there was enough to go round. I do wish you and Daddy had been there to have some of it, and I wish you were on this boat right now. I'm sure you would like it. There are two lovely bars! (Tee-hee!) I'm too far away for you to spank me now, and anyway I'm much too old for that kind of thing (I hope).

The crew of this ship are very kind and obliging – much nicer than the crew of the other one. The accommodation is very good, and the food is marvellous. I'll have to weigh myself at the next port I think. I'm sure this trip would have done Daddy the world of good, because they seem to cater for dispeptics (I hope I've spelt it right).

Talking of dispeptics, how are you keeping these days, dear grandpapa? I do hope the gout, rheumatism and housemaids knee are a little better. How is the prickly heat? I hope it's better too. Lots of people have it on this ship, but I haven't had any yet, although it has been very hot lately, especially at night. We are lucky in having a cabin to ourselves. Goodness knows what we would do if we had to share one. We're hoping and praying we will be lucky on the next ship, but I doubt it.

Before I end this letter, I have a confession to make. Guess what I did on my birthday? I went in the bar! Yes, I did, and what's more I sat on one of the stools round the counter and drank...All right, relax, it was only lime juice. Mummy was there too, so it's not quite as bad as it sounds, and I was only there a quarter of an hour and went to bed at 9.15. Actually we only went in the bar because we couldn't get a drink anywhere else, and they had to drink my health on my birthday. I didn't really like it there, but I just did it to be daring so that I could say I went into a bar on my sixteenth birthday and give you all a shock. I can imagine you all sitting down, shaking your heads and saying, "Such a pity that one so young should have started on the downward path. Why did we ever let her out of our sight?"

It is just over two weeks since we left Colombo, and it seems like two years. You all seem so far away now, and Mummy and I have quite lost count of what you are doing because we keep on having to put the clock back every night. We often think of you and wonder what you are doing, especially in the evenings when we miss you most. I miss our after-dinner walks a lot. It's horrible having to walk one's dinner down alone! Mummy and I always feel very morbid after dinner. I suppose it's because we used to have fun then in Colombo. I always thought it was the nicest part of the day because everyone was more cheery and there was a nice atmosphere.

Do you still look for the plough? I can find it myself now, but I prefer being shown it. It's much nicer! Ahem! Lovely weather we've been having lately, haven't we? What is the weather like in Colombo? Has the monsoon arrived yet? I suppose it rains a lot now and you are probably using your Mackintosh quite a lot.

[*This reminiscence about after dinner moonlight strolls along the beach in Colombo, particularly the part about Steve showing*

Molly the stars, is why I believe that it was on one of these walks that these two had their first kiss. Molly has a habit in her letters of changing the subject when she refers to affairs of the heart. She uses the word ahem, then starts writing about the weather. She had to be careful as she knew that the Naval Censor read everything. It was such a small tight-knit community that the censor could easily have been a colleague of Steve's, or worse still, her father's.]

How is our dear friend Mr W? I mustn't say too much because you never know who reads these letters. I'm sorry about the last letter and I'll be more careful in future. [*Steve must have told Molly off for her previous letter when she tactlessly revealed that Mr W was in fact Mr Wilson, Steve's difficult boss.]*

Anyway, I do hope things are better for you now. When I am writing letters to you and Daddy I often wonder if you will ever get them. It's a morbid thought I know, but I can't help it crossing my mind. Well, anyway, let's hope that this one reaches you safely. I really must stop now, so I'll say cheerio until the next time.

All my love, Molly xxxxxxx

[In Molly's diary she records that there were two calm days at sea before they arrived in Mombasa, East Africa, now Kenya. As there was no room in the harbour, they had to go on to the island of Zanzibar, escorted by a destroyer.]

May 10th

Arrived at Zanzibar. It seems to be a very pretty place and we are rather amused at the natives diving for pennies. They keep the money in their mouths when they dive and never seem to lose any of it.

May 11th

We were all allowed ashore in the morning, but were very disappointed in the place. There seems to be no main shopping centre, and the few shops there charge the most extortionate prices. After wandering around for about two hours we came back to the ship, but after lunch we received an invitation, through the Purser, from a Dr and Mrs Taylor asking four of us to tea. Mummy, Mrs Flinton, Mrs Wright and I went. They were very nice to us, and after tea took us for a drive around the island which is very pretty and picturesque. On the whole, a very nice day.

May 12th

Woken up very early in the morning, at about 4am, by the most terrific din – various people on board had been celebrating the barman's birthday, and none of them went to bed until about 5am. They all had very thick heads the next day, and very few turned up for breakfast.

The Chief Justice of Zanzibar invited all the children on board out for the day, and I went as well. We hope to get away tomorrow, but judging by the amount of coal there is waiting to come on board, it doesn't seem very likely.

May 13th

A very nice day indeed, today. Mrs Flinton, Mr Chase, James Hughes and myself went ashore to play tennis and had a very good game. After dinner there was dancing and everyone enjoyed themselves. Charles made us roar with laughter. He dressed up in his tails and absolutely acted the goat. He really is a scream. Haven't had so much fun for ages.

May 14th

Left Zanzibar for Mombasa where we are going to pick up some troops. The sea was quite rough and lots of people felt sick, including myself. I didn't dance, but went to bed early.

May 15th

Arrived at Mombasa at about 8am. Spent most of the morning on deck with the twins and Charles watching all the new passengers embarking. They didn't look a very inspiring crowd and we had some fun pulling them all to pieces. Most of them are RAF people and army officers. We weren't allowed ashore, worse luck. I was rather sorry because it looked a very pretty place – beautifully green and verdant. Mummy wanted more Rinso [*crossed out*] Lux for washing our clothes, so when Parsons (who was the only one excepting Charles allowed ashore) went ashore, he brought back about six packets which he sold to all the ladies on board. He did quite a roaring trade.

It took nearly the whole morning for the troops to embark – there seem to be quite a number of them, but at last they were all on board and we left at about one o'clock. The next stop will be Durban, thank goodness. We are very anxious to get there in case there is a letter or something for us from Daddy.

As we left, there was a bit of excitement. All the ships – there seemed to be thousands of them – saluted us as we sailed out. It was awfully inspiring and I was frightfully thrilled. There were so many big battleships and cruisers there that it looked just like Navy Week.

We attempted to dance after dinner, much to the amusement of all the new passengers, but they stared so much we decided to stop.

May 16th

Nothing very interesting happened today. The new crowd on board have rather spoilt it. All the army officers seem to do is play cards and smoke, and it's terribly difficult to get a game of deck quoits or shuffleboard because they bag all the courts. It's awful to even try and walk around the deck because it's so full of people, but we did manage to dance.

A ship
Still at sea
Sunday, May 17th 1942

Dear Steve,

(Excuse somewhat frigid beginning, but I never know how to begin your letters).

Well, here we are, still ploughing around the ocean and not getting very far, in spite of being practically a month at sea. We have been doing lots of strange things since I last wrote to you, and have been delayed quite a lot at various places. I expect you are all wondering what on earth the ship we are on is doing, and if this letter wasn't going to be censored, I could tell you quite a lot about our adventures in different places, but as it's wartime I'll just have to content myself with leaving out the names of the places we have been to and telling you what we did while we were at them.

You will probably have received the letter I posted to you from the second last port of call, and you will know the name of the place by the stamp, or at least I think you will. We stayed there for three days and went ashore every day. It wasn't much of a place for shops, but the people there were very hospitable indeed and gave us a jolly good time. The first day we were there, we had an invitation to tea from a Dr and his wife whom, of course, we didn't know at all.

The next day, the Chief Justice and his wife asked all the

children on board to their house for the day. I wasn't going to go in the beginning, not being a child (please note), but as both the Simmonds went, I went along as well. Now I'm glad I did, because we really had a grand time. First of all they took us to the Museum, and then we went to the house for a simply wonderful lunch. I won't go into all the details because it might make you hungry, especially if you still get the same sort of lunches you used to have when we were in Colombo.

I hope you have more time to eat now and that you aren't so busy. I feel dreadful when I think of you and Daddy working so hard while we are just enjoying ourselves and doing very little work. I do wish you were on this boat. We could have such fun. Actually I have been having quite a good time during the last few days because we have got to know more people on board, and they are quite a decent crowd on the whole.

While we were in port we had dancing every night, which was quite good fun. I think I told you there are some twins on board. Their names are James and Richard Hughes, and they are very much alike. I can tell which is which now, but I couldn't at first, and some people can't tell them apart yet. It's rather awkward sometimes, because I am never quite sure which one I danced with last. They are going all the way to England as well, and I'm quite glad because they are the only ones anywhere near my own age, and even then they are four years older. I'm hoping that we get a few more women and children at the next port, because at the moment we are just swamped with men, having collected a lot more at the last port.

I nearly forgot to tell you that I managed to get a game of tennis in at one port. In fact, I played five sets altogether and then came home and danced until 11.30 without stopping. What do you think of that for energy? There is life in the old dog yet, you see! I think that day was the best

I have had since we left Colombo. Tennis and dancing are two of my favourite things – and two of your pet aversions, aren't they? I've always regretted not being able to make you dance, but there's still time yet! You wait until I come home. I'll have you doing the tango, the rumba, and even la conga like a two-year-old, so look out!

This letter probably sounds as though I am living an idle and dissipated life, but actually it isn't as bad as it sounds. I've been slacking a bit over the shorthand and typing lately, but I started again this morning, and I have nearly finished the dress I am making and hope to wear it when we get to ------. This is annoying, honestly. I was just going to write down the name of the place, but I'll have to say the usual thing: 'when we get to the next port'. We are both very anxious to get there, because we are hoping for some news of Daddy and because we simply must buy some clothes and various things like soap and shampoos. We've just run out of everything.

[*Molly mentions to Steve that she and Ciss met a friend of Steve's father and hopes that his ship will call at Colombo so that Steve can meet him.*]

Colombo is such a long way away now, and by the time you get this letter so many other things will have happened. It's a dreadful feeling, you know, to think that we are getting further and further away, but I suppose it's all for the best, and we might all meet again quite soon. Let's hope so, anyway! Cheerio for the time being. BBC is now closing down. Xxxxxxx

May 17th

Weather is getting very rough now and Mrs Simmonds is in bed feeling very sea-sick. She always feels sick. Managed to have some dancing in spite of the weather. It's great fun really. The floor comes up to meet you one minute and rolls away from you the next. We lurched all over the place, but enjoyed ourselves just the same. I'm not feeling actually sick, but I feel as though I might be if it gets any rougher.

May 18th

The weather is even worse today. It's bitterly cold and very rough. As we were taking a walk around the deck after breakfast the sea came right up, and two or three passengers got a wetting. The deck was terribly wet and slippery so we couldn't walk very much. Rather a miserable day on the whole. Nobody seems inclined to do much, and I don't feel at all good. The food is getting pretty rotten now because no one expected to have these troops on board, so the result is there isn't so much to eat as there was. Didn't dance after dinner – felt too queer. Shall be very glad when we reach Durban, although I am enjoying this trip immensely. The crowd we go around with are a very jolly lot and I do hope we all get transhipped together. It would be rotten if we got put on separate ships.

May 19th

Weather is still very cold and rough. Wore my slacks, a jumper and a blazer all day and still felt cold. B-r-r-h! Danced after dinner and we all had our fortunes told by Mrs. Simmonds. It was jolly good fun, but rather embarrassing at times. I had my leg pulled well and truly by the twins, but I got my own back afterwards by teasing them about their fortunes.

May 20th

Arrived in Durban [South Africa] at about three o'clock in the afternoon. It looks a marvellous place from the sea with some immense skyscrapers along the sea front. As there are so many ships in the docks we cannot land today – there is no place for the ship to berth in. We shall probably go alongside tomorrow. I hope so anyway because I'm longing to get ashore and see all the shops.

It was bitterly cold after dinner on deck, and for once I was glad of the blanket in bed. It is winter in Durban now and all the officers and ratings are wearing their blues. They look much nicer than the whites.

May 21st

Went alongside at about 11am. The health officer and a customs official came on board and we had to obtain landing permits before going ashore. Said goodbye to all the crew of the ship. We are all very, very sorry to leave it because we have had a lovely trip and will always look back on it with pleasure.

Went ashore at about two o'clock to go to the Naval Office where we were told a cable is waiting for us. I wonder what it contains…

Gloucester Hotel
St Andrew's Street
Durban

23rd May 1942

Well, here I am again. Please excuse my writing in pencil, but I have lost my pen, and in any case there is such a lot to tell you so I must write very fast.

To begin with, as you can see by this address, we are staying in digs in Durban. We had a signal from Daddy to remain here until further instructions came for us. At first we were jolly pleased, or at least Mummy was very pleased, but I had rather mixed feelings about it all because, as you know, I really want to go home badly. Now we don't feel so good about it, and in fact we are absolutely fed up and miserable once more.

The trouble is, you see, that we don't know whether Daddy is coming on here or not, and even when he is coming. If he doesn't come within the next three weeks we shall be absolutely stony broke because the hotel we are staying in at present is charging five guineas a week for us both, and even then we are sharing a room with Mrs Wright who travelled with us from Colombo. If we took it on a monthly basis it would be cheaper, but we are afraid to do that because we don't know how long we will be here. Mummy and I are of course the odd men out again, because although all the other people who travelled with us are staying in digs as well, they at least know that they have only to remain here a few days until a boat arrives, whereas we just have to stay put for goodness knows how long.

Mummy is nearly frantic with worry because she can't see how we are going to live here, and we both wish that that signal had never been sent. Of course we want to see Daddy and don't mind waiting here for him, but it doesn't state definitely that he is coming, although we can't see any other reason for our being detained here. This place is poisonously dear and we want millions of things because it is midwinter and we both feel the cold terribly, but we are afraid to buy anything because we shan't have enough money to pay the rent. There is no Lloyds Bank here, but luckily Barclays Bank has granted us an advance of £20, which I suppose is better than nothing. If Daddy doesn't come soon we don't know what we shall do, because when the others go on in the next boat we shall hardly know a soul.

You remember I mentioned a Lieut. Chase whom we knew in Deal? Well, he has been terribly kind to us, and goodness knows what we will do when he goes. We have only been here two days and in that time we have been out twice. Guess where I went the night we arrived? I'm getting awfully bad! I went to a night club with Charlie Chase, Mummy and one of the twins I told you about before. It was quite an experience, but I didn't really like it very much. It was awfully hot and stuffy and the smoke made my eyes smart, and there were so many people dancing that it was impossible to do anything more than shuffle around. We stayed until they started singing some rather doubtful songs, and then we decided it was time we went.

We have just heard that all the other people are going tomorrow and we are all feeling fed up to the back teeth. It seems as though we are fated to be left behind every time. This is our second disappointment, but if only I knew we were going on to England I wouldn't mind waiting here for ages. If we have to stay in this beastly hole, after setting our hearts on going home, it will be the end of everything. I'm awfully sorry to be writing you such a depressing letter, but it does relieve my feelings. I expect you are just as depressed, but I hope not.

If only we could see somebody like you or Daddy walking down the street, I think we would go off our heads with joy. Perhaps you have been appointed somewhere else. Wouldn't it be marvellous if you came here? I'm sure you would like it. It is exactly like England in everything and the climate is marvellous. I'll tell you more about it in my next letter, because I really must stop now as it is lunchtime. I'll write again soon. Cheerio!

Tons and tons of love from Molly
xxxxxxxxxxxxxxxxxxxxxxxxxxxxx

In the last-minute dash to leave Colombo, Don had given Ciss enough money for incidentals to tide her over until she reached England. On the ship their board and lodging had been included in the price of the fare. But a last minute change of plan by the Admiralty, redeploying Don to an as yet secret destination, meant Molly and Ciss were to stay in South Africa until further notice. In a foreign country with not a penny to their name, the situation was about to get worse.

CHAPTER 7
– CASTLES IN THE AIR

Three weeks later, Molly and Ciss are still in Durban in the same hotel, living three to a room. Their financial situation is so desperate they spend their days window-shopping and their evenings in their hotel room, where Molly writes letters. Steve is one of the few people she can confide in.

Gloucester Hotel
118 St Andrew's Street
Durban

13th June 1942

Dearest Nunc,

I expect you have received my last letter by now. I really must apologise for it. Remember the moaning letters I used to send you from school and when we first went to Colombo? I'm sure they cheered you up no end. Well, at any rate, this letter is going to be more cheerful (I hope) and I have quite a bit of news to tell you.

We have been here three weeks now, but of course it seems much longer. This hotel is quite a decent place and the people have thawed a bit now. They do speak to us occasionally, which is something, I suppose. Mummy and I are still pretty down in the dumps, but now we know that

Daddy is leaving Colombo, and that there is a chance of our joining him soon, we feel a bit better. I know Mummy does at any rate. I'm afraid I'm horribly disappointed because we aren't going home [*to England*]. In fact, when we received Daddy's letter I just felt as if the bottom had dropped out of everything.

I'm afraid I said some awful things about him – there wasn't a name I didn't call him, but now of course I realise what a rotten time he has had without us, and what a state his mind must have been in, trying to know what to do for the best. Don't repeat this, but Mummy and I are furious with Susie and Robbie for making him leave Melbourne Avenue.

[*When Ciss and Molly were evacuated from Colombo, Don gave them all the money he had. Their finances were tight, yet the Robertsons still expected Don to pay them the same rent and board he'd been paying for the three of them.*]

I suppose they had to charge him extra for a good reason, but personally I think they are jolly mean. They might have stretched a point when they knew what a mess he was in, but perhaps I don't know what I'm talking about, so I'd better not air my opinions too much.

I haven't written to Daddy at all since we arrived here, because I'm afraid I shall start saying nasty things when I really ought to thank him for doing what, I suppose, will turn out for the best. This letter sounds very Bolshevik, and unreasonable, but it's mild to what I would have written a week ago. They say time heals all wounds, so I hope that in another week's time I shall be able to write a nice letter to Daddy instead of a nasty one.

We are staying in this hotel until such time as we hear of Daddy's arrival in Mombasa, and then we are hoping he will send for us. I'm sure you and Daddy would love it here, because it's very much like England. I still can't get over seeing so many white faces in the streets. It doesn't seem right somehow. Instead of seeing buses and streets full of milling natives, one sees crowds and crowds of white people. It still gives me quite a thrill to see all the English shops with English shopgirls (or rather, South African), but they are white, and so are all the bus drivers and bus conductors. They have women bus conductors here, and women taxi-drivers as well. It's very puzzling to know quite how to treat them. We are not allowed to call the table boys 'boy' here. They get very annoyed unless you address them as 'waiter' and I'm always getting ticked off for saying, 'boy'. Oh well, I suppose I'll get used to it soon.

[*This is the first time Molly had encountered white working class South Africans. After five years abroad she may have forgotten what it was like in the shops back in England.*]

At the moment I am going to the Convent High School for shorthand and typing, but they break up at the end of the month, and I'm not sure what I shall do then. It depends on Daddy's cable. If we have to stay here for some time then I'm off to get a job as soon as I can. I think it's about time I started being a help instead of a hindrance to the family. The trouble is that I'm not really fit for anything. My shorthand will pass (I did 90 words a minute last week, but that was only because it was an easy passage), but my typing's very weak. I don't know the first thing about book-keeping or filing or anything, and you know what a head I've got for figures. Still, I'm determined to do something, and it's all experience. Just think what a shock Daddy will get if I do manage to get a job. They are easy enough to get here and the salaries are quite good, but don't tell Daddy anything about it, will you, because it probably won't come off.

[*If she'd had the opportunity, Molly would have dearly loved to have carried on with English and History, the subjects she'd enjoyed so much at school, but her hopes of going on to higher education were starting to fade. Shorthand and typing skills were useful, and in peacetime might have led to a career in journalism or publishing. In wartime, the best she could hope for was a job as a secretary.*]

Another reason why I very much doubt that I'll get a job is that I don't look the part. If only I had some decent grown-up looking clothes, it would be easy. I've got a pair of silk stockings now, you know. It's the first pair I've ever had and they do feel funny. I like the silky feeling about my legs. It makes me feel luxurious and expensive, although they only cost 1/11. I get quite a kick out of wearing them, and I'm doing so at the present moment. (By the way, I don't think it is very good form to discuss things like silk stockings with ones male acquaintances ('male acquaintance' does sound grand, doesn't it) so I hope you don't mind).

Mummy has bought me a lovely new coat and a pair of shoes, so I have one warm thing that is respectable. I have been living in my school things ever since we arrived and now I just hate the sight of them. Ugh! Everyone else is so smart and Mummy and I are so shabby, it's most annoying. That's one of the reasons why I want to work. When I draw my first month's salary, I'm going to give half to Mummy and we're going to spend it all on clothes. Hurrah! Gosh, will we enjoy ourselves.

You should see the list I've written out for Daddy of the things I want. I know I shan't get any of them, but it's almost as much fun to write them all out and plan them as it is to buy them. If we stay here I shall have to have about three winter frocks, a skirt, lots of stockings and shoes and jumpers and another suit. What colour do you suggest for the suit?

I forgot to describe my coat to you! It is a very light beige with brown leather buttons and it is very smart. It looks something like this. No good, I can't draw. I'll send you a snap of myself in it. I think you will like it. Everyone else does, anyway. At the moment I am wearing a little brown skull cap stuck at the back of my head with it, but I want a nice brown hat really, and, of course, brown shoes, brown gloves, a brown scarf and a flower for my button-hole. Then I shall be quite respectable. If we stay here, Mummy is having my grey school skirts altered and I'm going to have a scarlet jacket or jersey to wear with them, so that I will have another outfit. (All this will probably never happen, but it's nice to build castles in the air).

Daddy told me in his letter that you are still working terribly hard, and that you don't get home until eight o'clock at night sometimes. Surely they can't make you work as hard as all that? It isn't fair to pile all the work on to one man. If I were you I would pretend I was ill or something, but I know you wouldn't do that because you are too conscientious. Anyway, I do hope that by the time you get this letter things will be much better. Do you think there is any chance of you being transferred to where Daddy is going? Wouldn't it be marvellous if you were! You couldn't keep me away from it then! They say it is a pretty awful place, but it couldn't possibly be any worse than Colombo. In any case it's the people in a place that make it good or bad, not the place itself. (That's rather a back-handed compliment, seeing I have just said that no place could be worse than Colombo, but I hope you get me.)

Do you like it any better now? I hope you do, because it's rotten having to live in a place you don't like. We weren't there long enough to get to like it properly, and except that we had to leave you and Daddy behind, Mummy and I aren't at all sorry that we left. We really think that we would like it here if only Daddy would come and we could have a home of our own again. Hotel life is horrid! If we had a little flat we would be much happier.

[*Molly goes on to tell Steve that she has met up with a friend, Muriel Squibb, who was a fellow pupil at CBS (Central British School) in Hong Kong. Muriel and Molly have a good time gossiping about mutual friends and acquaintances.*]

Another thing I like about Muriel is that she doesn't go out with or know any boys. It's such a change to talk to someone who isn't always jabbering about boyfriends and what they do and how wonderful they are, etc., etc. The girls at school really make me sick because they can talk of nothing else, and Muriel says that's why she hasn't made any friends here.

Unfortunately Mummy is trying to hurry me up because she wants me to go for a walk. She sends you her love and says she misses you a lot and is always 'dreaming of thee'. That's what she said, anyway.

We have just received another cable and some letters from Daddy. He at last appears to be moving, so now we are hoping that he is on his way to Mombasa. We are just waiting for a cable to tell us of his arrival, and then we will know what to do.

Daddy says you received our cable alright. I expect you were jolly surprised to get it. We didn't know what to do because we thought Daddy had left, but weren't really sure. Heaven knows why we didn't think of cabling you before, but we were in such a flummox that it didn't occur to us. I suppose all this will seem very funny when we look back upon it, but it doesn't strike any of us that way at present, although we do have a good laugh occasionally.

Mrs Wright used to work with Mummy in Singapore, and she travelled all the way down with us and was in pretty much the same position as ourselves when we arrived. We decided to share a room – more for economy than anything else, because at that time we didn't quite know where the next penny was coming from. The room we are in isn't really big enough for three, but we manage.

It has been freezingly cold here just lately and sometimes I don't know what to do to keep warm. I go round huddled up in all the woollies I can find and I'm getting quite round-shouldered from hunching my shoulders and putting my hands (which are always cold) into my pockets. I even had a hot water bottle for my feet the other night because they are generally like two blocks of ice. We have all got chapped lips and faces from the cold and my nose is now an even brighter and shinier shade of red than it was in Colombo. Added to all these attractions, my hair is coming out in handfuls every time I comb it, so on the whole I am a picture no artist could paint.

(Figure 7.1, Molly's drawing of her falling out hair, red nose, perpetually drooping lips, and her remarks about her round shoulders and increasing waistline from eating too much, can be viewed in the gallery section of the website: http://www.lambertnagle.com)

Of course I had a cold after I arrived here, but actually I am feeling a lot better since and am eating like a horse. I've lost my appetite and found a donkey's, and everyone says I look a lot better. Mummy looks better too, but she still worries a lot and can't sleep at nights. This is worrying me a bit because we've got enough trouble at the moment without her wearing herself out. She wanted to start work again in the cipher office, but thank goodness I managed to talk her out of it. The hours here are even worse than they were in Colombo [*the ciphering shifts were not only long, but often involved working overnight*], and I know Daddy would be furious if he knew she was doing that work again when he sent her away for a holiday.

[*This, along with one other reference to Ciss's ciphering, is the only proof I have of the work that she did for the Admiralty. Like so many of the other wives, Ciss played a vital but sadly now forgotten role in the overseas section of the Bletchley Park operation*].

She says we could do with the money to buy new clothes, but if anyone's got to work it will be me this time. At the moment she is taking a typing course, so that if we do go to

Mombasa, she will be able to work in the 'Loony Bin' like Mrs Townsend, etc.

[*Roland H Worth, in his book Secret Allies in the Pacific: Covert Intelligence and Code Breaking, writes that those who worked in FECB did call it the 'Loony Bin', presumably because of the intense pressure of their intelligence work.*]

I am writing this letter on my knee at the moment because the air raid siren has just gone and of course we are all blacked out. I don't know whether it's a practice or not, but I hope it isn't the real thing because it would be the last straw if we started having air raids here.

[*Fortunately this air raid was a precaution as Durban itself was not in fact bombed, although many ships were torpedoed off the South African coast.*]

Tons and tons of love and xxs from Molly
xxxxxxxxxxxxxxxxxxxxxxxxx

P.S. How about writing to me? I haven't had a letter from you at all yet.

It is not until 28 June 1942, two weeks later, that Molly writes another letter to Steve from the Gloucester Hotel.

My dear Steve,

Well, at last I have received a letter from you, and I should think it is about time too. (Consider yourself ticked off, young man.) Actually I don't mean it, but I thought I'd give you a fright. (Have I?)

I'm glad you like the new form of address, and I'm very pleased to think that it makes you feel younger. If you really want to feel younger still, I'll start my next letter with 'Darling ickle Steviekins', and end up with 'Lots of love and bear hugs from Auntie'. Would you like that? Somehow I don't think you would.

Judging by your letter you seem to have been working

terribly hard, and I suppose you still are. How awful having to work on Saturdays and Sundays as well. It was awfully sweet of you to write to me on your first Sunday off, but honestly you shouldn't have bothered. I'm jolly mean asking you to write when I know you're so busy, so don't take any notice of my last two letters where I've dropped nasty hints about some people not writing to other people. I was just being selfish. All I think about is that I love getting letters from you, quite forgetting that you have very little time to write them in.

I do hope by now that you have found someone else to feed the coolies [*she uses the word here to mean labourers*] for you, and that you don't have to rush all over Ceylon looking for rice for them. Does Mr Hall still trade in elephants? It always makes me laugh when I think of him riding on an elephant. He must look funny! I expect you would look funny too, and I'm sure I'd look even funnier.

I still go to school for shorthand and typing. I have been going to the Convent, but as they have broken up for their winter holidays, I now go to the Technical School with Mummy for a special vacation course. All the schools are on holiday now and the place is crowded with trippers from Johannesburg and all the towns upcountry.

Durban is exactly like an English holiday resort. It reminds me of Brighton in lots of ways. There is a marvellous beach and esplanade, and everything is so English-if-ied I can't get over it. All the shops here are absolutely marvellous. You can get anything you want in Woolworths and there are lots of bazaars and things. The dress shops are wonderful. Mummy and I spend half our time looking in the windows at all the creations and wishing we could buy them. Last week we went hunting for a frock for me, but we were rather unsuccessful as they were all too big, except one which was just the right length but a bit too tight. I am putting on weight in this place, and have actually grown again. I'm nearly as tall as Mummy in my shoes, and all my Colombo frocks have been let down. (I expect they'll have to be let out soon if I don't stop eating so much.) I was weighed and measured last week and am seven stone four and five foot and half an inch in my socks, but five foot two and a quarter in my shoes. If you don't believe me, I've got it written down in black and white on the card.

Mummy is looking a lot better since she has been here. I think the change is doing her good, and she is getting proper rest and food now. I hope we don't have to stay here, though, because if we do, she says she's going to start ciphering again, and if there's anything I don't want her to do, it's that.

We have had a cable from Daddy saying that he is in Mombasa and is doing his best to get us there. All we are waiting for now is a cable telling us to go. Now that we can't go home I'm completely indifferent as to where we go. One place is as good as any other. Daddy is the only reason why I want to go to Mombasa. There's nobody else there that I want to see.

I suppose there is no chance of you being transferred there? Wouldn't it be marvellous if you were there! As you say in your letter, there's bound to be a third place, so why shouldn't it be Mombasa? There's supposed to be one or two decent shops and a nice golf course, and I believe you can get lots of riding there too. We have been there twice on the way here, as you know, but we never managed to get ashore.

You seem to be very curious about my fortune in your letter, so perhaps I'll disclose a little more (but not all). I've had it told three times since I left Colombo. Once by an Indian at Bombay, once by Mrs Simmonds and once by a girl here who reads tea cups. Of course I don't believe in them, but it's rather fun listening to what they say.

You should have heard the old Indian at Bombay. He

talked a lot of tripe about two people being madly in love with me and said I was going to be very rich and happy and all the rest of it, but I didn't take any notice of that because he told three other people exactly the same. One thing he said rather annoyed me because I suppose it hurt my pride. He said I was very good. but rather cunning. I didn't like the bit about being cunning. Perhaps it's true, although I don't think I am.

Coming down on the ship, [*we*] all had our fortunes told by Mrs Simmonds. She reads cards and is supposed to be quite good. All that she told me has come true up to now, and I hope all the rest does! It is most uncanny how everything she has told both Mummy and me has turned out. You see, she told me that I wasn't going home but would stay in Durban, and then take a short journey with a fair woman (of course, meaning Mummy). We hope the short journey will be to Mombasa. She said that we would hear of a move made by a man between dark and fair, and of course that means Daddy, and she said lots of other things as well. It got quite embarrassing in the end, because of course the twins [*James and Richard Hughes*] were there listening with both ears, and I got my leg pulled like anything. Still, I got my own back by listening in to theirs and teasing them.

Another thing that Mrs Simmonds said was that I would hear of a marriage in the family, and of course we have just heard that my uncle Clarence [*Don's younger brother*] has got married. I'm awfully annoyed because he's my favourite uncle and I was looking forward to seeing him. I've had a pash on him for ages and now he's gone and spoilt it all by getting married. Anyway, I hope his wife will keep him in order. It will serve him right if she does. (Sour grapes, aren't I?)

[*Molly mentions mutual acquaintances from Singapore days, both of whom are now in various parts of South Africa.*]

I suppose it is terribly hot now in Colombo and the rainy

season has pretty well set in. It must be an awful nuisance getting to and from work in the rain, but I expect your mac comes in handy. I hope it doesn't leak like mine does. How do you get to work now? Do you still go in the car or have you bought a bike yet? I'm hoping Daddy hasn't sold mine because I shall want it if we go to Mombasa.

Today is Sunday and we went for a lovely drive. [*A kind couple they knew in Singapore staying at their hotel took Molly and Ciss out to see the countryside.*] I think South Africa is a beautiful country because it reminds me of England so much. Even the sweet shops have that nice English-y smell. We saw some marvellous houses today and I have chosen the one I want to live in. It isn't big and it isn't small, but just right. It has a lovely big garden with a lawn and a rockery, is covered with ivy in front and has a little porch with a dear little lamp hanging in it, but I'm not quite sure whether I like its latticed windows best or the big bay windows of another house I saw. I love bay windows with lots of seats and cushions, don't you? When I win the Irish Sweep or the Grand National, that's the sort of house I'll have, except that I shall have to add a tennis court and kennels and stables for the dogs and horses.

Yesterday the July Handicap was run here. All the people from Jo'berg and upcountry came down for it and there was an awful to-do. Everyone has been full of the races for the last week. We had a sweepstake in the hotel, and I drew a horse. His name was Thermos, but I'm afraid the poor old thing came in tenth. All my horses do. Do you remember the one I named after you at school when we used to play horse racing? He came in tenth as well. It's a pity Thermos didn't win because the first prize was £10 and that would have done Mummy and I very nicely.

We nearly die of boredom in the evenings because there is nothing to do. It isn't safe to go out in the blackout so we just sit at home and vegetate. Mummy says if something doesn't happen soon, she'll go completely scats. I have been reduced to knitting and have at last learnt how to knit properly. Isn't it disgraceful that I couldn't knit before? But I'm afraid it's true. Still, I can knit now, and am getting on like a house on fire with a jumper for myself which I'm going to embroider when it is finished. Mummy is very rude about my efforts and says the war will be over before I've finished, but I intend to surprise her by finishing it next week. If we stay here and take a flat I shall have to do the cooking and then look out for squalls [*tantrums*]. I'll ask you to dinner if you ever come here. What a horrible fate!

I hope the next letter I write will be from Mombasa. Of course, it would be ten times better if I didn't have to write another letter to you at all, but could see you instead. I miss you an awful lot, honestly, and although it's lovely to get letters from you, they don't make up for my not being able to see you. I've been hoping and hoping that you will come to Mombasa because I just can't believe that I'm not going to see you again for years and years. It's a morbid thought, but unless you are transferred to Mombasa, there doesn't seem a hope of ever seeing you until we go home, and even then you mightn't be there. I suppose I'm being very cheerful and I am sure you are being cheered up no end, so I will keep my thoughts to myself.

Don't take any notice of what I have just written, because I didn't write this letter with the intention of being miserable, and I'm still hoping that you'll come to Mombasa or somewhere in South Africa. At any rate, I do hope you'll get moved from Colombo, or if you do have to stay there, that you will like it better. Don't forget to write back soon – it need only be a page or something – if you have a spare minute. You had better write to me C/O Daddy. I suppose you know his address.

I must stop now, so I'll say cheerio for the present! Here's hoping we meet again soon!

Tons and tons of love and xxs from Molly

xxxxxxxxxxxxxxxxxxxxxxxxxxxxxxxxxxxxxxxxxxxxxxxxx

Molly doesn't write again to Steve for another six weeks. They're still in Durban, staying at the same hotel, but in this letter there's been a reversal of fortune and life is about to take a turn for the better.

4th August '42

My dearest, darling, most spiffing Steve!

Forgive this mad beginning, but at the moment I feel so happy I could throw my arms around and embrace everyone within range! If you were here, I'd give you a bear hug that would knock you flat and leave you breathless for a week. You don't know how deliriously happy I am. I feel as though I want to scream for joy and turn somersaults on the bed. Guess what has happened! We can go to Mombasa!!!! Whoopee!

If you only knew what an awful time we have had here for the last two months, you would understand why I am so thrilled that we will soon be together again. Honestly, during the past three weeks, when everything seemed so hopeless, I thought I should go mad. Mummy has worried me terribly because she is pining for Daddy all the time. She wouldn't eat or sleep or anything, and I don't think I've ever seen her so miserable. I have been the cheery one this time and kept on telling her that things would turn out all right, until last Friday when we received a letter from Daddy saying everything was hopeless and that we would have to resign ourselves to staying in Durban for the duration.

Then of course I came down with a bump. From Friday till this morning, the Lambert Waterworks Company did lots of work. They've done so much work lately that I wonder I have any eyes left, but that's beside the point. The main thing is that everything has turned out alright, and the sooner the miserable part of the business is forgotten, the better. Mummy has aged about ten years since we've been here, but this news will be like a tonic to her. She's looking tons better already.

Do you know, I don't think that people like Mummy and Daddy are meant to be separated, because neither of them can live without the other. I'm old enough to see that even I don't make up to Mummy for Daddy or vice versa. It's quite natural, and I'm terribly glad they aren't like some people's mothers and fathers, who don't care a hoot for each other. Last night I was so miserable that I wrote to you and told you all my troubles. You're the only person I can do that to without thinking that I'll be laughed at or thought stupid. When I had finished the letter I felt tons better for having 'unburdened my soul' on paper, although I felt rather guilty about sending it to you when you have enough troubles of your own. Still, as I've said before, you shouldn't be so nice and understanding and sympathetic. It's lucky you are, though, because I don't know what I should do if you weren't. Anyway, thank goodness I have torn it up now, and can write a cheerful letter for once in my life.

First of all I must thank you for your cable, which arrived with Daddy's. I'm so glad they came together, although at first when I saw yours I had a bit of a scare because I thought something had happened. It was terribly sweet of you to send it, and it gave me quite a thrill. Imagine my having a cable all to myself! It made me feel quite ten years older. I suppose the letter you received when you cabled was the awful one I wrote in pencil. I'm terribly sorry about that. It was an awful cheek to send it like that, but at the time I felt so desperate that I hardly knew what I was doing.

I am sending this letter by Air Mail as I think the occasion deserves 3d for a stamp. Isn't it dreadful? We've been so broke that I couldn't afford to send your letters by Air Mail before. However, when I am earning my own living, I shall be so rich that I'll be able to send cables every day. Just you watch me!

Mr Cousins [*Don's colleague*] has at last arrived here and came round to see us on Sunday. That was when we thought we wouldn't see Daddy until the end of the war, and of course seeing all the Cousins united made us feel terribly jealous. In fact when I met Mr Cousins I disgraced myself entirely by practically sobbing on his shoulder. Still, in spite of wishing he were Daddy, and being green with envy of Muriel and Mrs Cousins, Mummy and I were very pleased to see him because he had been with Daddy so much in Colombo.

He told us quite a lot about Daddy and made us laugh with stories of how they used to do their own mending, etc. He said they used to iron their hankies and vests and things between two books. You taught them that, didn't you? We heard one or two stories of nights at the Swimming Club that made us think that perhaps things weren't so bad after we left. Still, we realise that you only did it to 'drown your sorrows' (Ahem!). Anyway, it's nice to hear that you did enjoy yourselves and I hope you are continuing to do so. I'm sure Daddy is, now that he knows we can soon join him.

In his letter today, he told me that you might come either to Durban or Mombasa. Oh, I do, do, wish you'll come to Mombasa. That would make everything perfect, because at the moment, Daddy is the only person that I care for in Mombasa. Daphne Carver is the only girl of my age that I know there, and from what Daddy has told me, I rather wish I didn't know her. Apparently she doesn't live with her parents any longer, but shares a flat or a room with another woman who is a bad influence on her. I have always liked Daphne and I never thought she was bad, really. She just seems to get in with the wrong people, and, of course, her parents don't even try and stop her. I'm glad my parents aren't like that (says she, proudly).

If you come to Durban, I shall be terribly annoyed, especially if you miss us, which you are almost certain to do.

Can't you try and wangle it so that you are sent to M? That is, of course, if you want to go there. It's not much of a place from all accounts, and except that Daddy is there, I'm not at all anxious to go. Durban is really much nicer as a town, but the only person here that I shall be sorry to leave behind is Muriel Squibb. She remembers you quite well and we often talk about you. Do your ears burn sometimes? Yesterday was August Bank Holiday and I spent the day at the Squibbs. They have a lovely home, right on the seafront, and I had the most marvellous lunch. Mrs Squibb is awfully sweet, and her cooking is nearly as good as Mummy's. It was such a treat to taste some home cooking. I get so sick of the food we get at this hotel. They never give you nice puddings or anything. (Aren't I a little piggy? Always talking about my tummy!)

We didn't do very much yesterday except listen to some concerts on the sea-front, but still we enjoyed ourselves quite a lot and it made a nice change. Muriel works, as I told you before, and she gets very few holidays.

Some other people in this hotel have been very kind to Mummy and I. They are a Mr and Mrs Russell. Mr Russell is English and very nice indeed, and Mrs Russell is Ygoslavian (how do you spell it?). She is very sweet too. In fact, they both have been terribly decent and I don't know what we should have done without them. They have a lovely car and have taken us for drives practically every weekend for the last six weeks. We have seen quite a lot of the surrounding countryside and have visited nearly all the beauty spots. South Africa is certainly a lovely country. The scenery is marvellous.

Last weekend we had a lovely surprise. I think I told you that the Coates are now living in Pietermaritzburg, which is about 50 miles from Durban. Well, on Saturday Mr Russell asked us if we would like to go for a drive to Maritzburg as neither he nor Mrs Russell had been there before, and they knew we had friends there and would like to see around the place. Of course, we jumped at the chance, and I hunted down one of Flora's letters to find out her address in case we could manage to see her.

We arrived at Maritzburg at about four o'clock and I phoned the Coates up to tell them that I was there. They nearly had a fit, or at least they sounded as though they were going to have one when I announced where I was. They live 3 miles out of the town in a terribly out-of-the-way place, and I'm sure it must be frightfully boring for them. They were as pleased as punch to see us and we were very glad to see them.

Flora is much the same as ever. She doesn't like it there, and I don't blame her. If I was stuck in a place like that, I would have gone crazy long ago. She says there is nothing to do there at all, except study. She is going to carry on studying to be a teacher and is going to the Convent at Maritzburg next term, lucky old hag. I wish I didn't have to work, but there's no help for it, I'm afraid.

Well, there's not much more space, so I'm afraid I'll have to stop now. Thank you once again for the cable. I do hope you'll go to M. I'm dying to see you again. If you knew the number of times Mummy and I have wished you were here during the last few awful weeks, you'd be quite flattered.

Tons and tons of love and bear hugs

From Molly

xxxxxxxxxxxxxxxxxxxxxxxxxxxxxxxxxxxxxxxxxxxxxxxxxxxxx
xxxxxxxxxxxxxxxxx

CHAPTER 8
– REUNITED IN EAST AFRICA

Molly and Ciss were finally given permission to travel to East Africa and arrived in Mombasa on 13 October, where the Eastern Fleet and the FECB had been relocated from Ceylon. There had been a big gap in Molly's letters to Steve because of the move.

Flat No 4
Raynor House
Mombasa
19th Oct '42

Dearest Steve,

As you can see by the address Mummy and I are at last in Mombasa, after waiting for four months to get here. I have piles of letters to answer, but I regard this one as the most important (get up and bow!). I am writing in a hurry, because now I am working (to be referred to later) I haven't a minute to myself. (This sounds as though I am absolutely indispensable, doesn't it? Actually I only started today.)

Anyway, we still don't know definitely whether we can actually stay here or not. I know it sounds ridiculous, because we are both employed here, but apparently the Civil Authorities have to reconsider the matter. The DC [*Deputy Commissioner*] here cannot do anything because the PC

[*Police Commissioner*] is away, but he very kindly gave us a temporary permit to stay in Mombasa until the PC comes back. Somehow I think everything will be alright because we shall both have been in jobs a fortnight and they can't push us off then. We've done all we can now. The rest is in the lap of the Gods. I will write again at the end of our term of sentence and tell you of our fate.

It is so nice to see all the familiar faces again after our exile in Durban. It feels like being back in Singapore (at least almost. There are still one or two faces missing that I should like to see).

I should like to know what is happening to you. The people in your department say you are going home, Daddy says you may go to South Africa, but no one seems to think you will come here. I only hope so, but it seems a pretty faint hope because I know that your department has too many people here already.

I expect you think I am talking in riddles, but I will attempt to clarify. Since I have been here, I have had the offer of no less than five jobs as a stenographer. (Daddy will go round telling people I'm so wonderful and all the rest of it, and I'm so frightened I shall let him down all the time I just can't do a thing. At least I couldn't today.) The day I arrived, people from the NSO, VSO Captain-on-Staff and your department all came up and wanted me to go along to their offices. You've no idea how short-staffed they are here. People are crying out for shorthand typists. Any poor mutt could get a job here. (That's why I got one).

Anyway, as your department asked first, I went along and did some typing for them the day after I arrived. Crumbs! I was shaking in my shoes! First of all I had to go and see Mr King (he knows you, so I expect you know him). He was quite nice and said that he would like me to be his stenographer. I would have loved to work for him because he seemed awfully decent, but as Daddy's department [*Captain-on-Staff – or Captain-on-Staff (HMS Sultan) to give its full cover identity – was really the office of the head of the intelligence monitoring unit: FECB*] have first claim on me, I have no choice. Still, I did some typing that afternoon and everyone was very nice to me. They laughed and cracked jokes when I made mistakes and made me feel quite at home. I was quite sorry to go home.

I think Daddy would rather I worked for one of the civilian departments, and I would definitely prefer it, especially now I have had a taste of what it is like to work for the other departments [*Molly had heard how pressured it was to work in intelligence*] (you know what I mean, I hope). Unfortunately, I have no choice in the matter at all because if I don't work for them they won't use their influence to help us get a permit to stay here permanently. It's a horrible position to be in, but later on I'm going to try and work for an outside firm. At present, though, I am thankful to be allowed to work for anyone.

I didn't expect to start for another few days. I have been helping Daddy for the last three or four days, but this afternoon I got the shock of my life when the phone went and I was told that I had to start work that afternoon. At the time I was feeling awful, having one of my nice colds again, and then I had to bicycle about 3 miles to reach Naval Headquarters, so by the time I arrived I was feeling too wonderful for words.

On top of that I had to sit down and do reams of typing and some shorthand for a person who didn't seem to realise that it was my first job and that I might be feeling just a little (ahem) nervous. (Actually I was quaking like a jelly and my hand wouldn't keep steady when I was taking down the shorthand. As a matter of fact it's wobbling now, but that's not nervousness – only old age.) I think he imagined I was a thought-reader or something because he just put things in front of me and expected me to get on with them.

Of course it was like so much Greek and I told him so, but it didn't seem to have much effect. Do you know how long he kept me working there? Until 5.30! Was I wild!!!! It's nothing to what Daddy was, though!

22nd October

Well, I didn't get time to finish this letter, being a hard-working woman now, but since then I have been working for three days and feel much happier about it. In fact, I feel as though I have been doing it all my life. It's awfully funny being called 'Miss Lambert' all the time instead of 'Molly', but it does make me feel old and grown-up and important. I wish you could see me dashing around with papers under my arm being efficient (or trying). It's really no good because I'm just as untidy and scatter-brained as ever – you ask Mummy – but I'm trying hard, and Daddy says I'll have to be tidy and not lose things in an office.

When we next meet, you won't know me. I shall be so tidy and prim and proper, and I shall hold out my hand and say politely, "How do-o you do, Mr Stephens. I think we have met somewhere before, have we not? Your face is very familiar." Would you like that, or would you prefer someone to let out a wild yell and nearly knock you over and strangle you with a most terrific bear hug? (Personally, I think it's a choice of two evils, don't you?)

I suppose you know we are living with the Bests for the time being. Mrs Best is hoping to go to New Zealand, and when she goes we are going to have her flat (always provided we are allowed to stay here, of course). I've definitely given up making plans and building castles in the air because they just don't work out (voice of experience speaking). Take your Granny's advice, my boy, and don't build castles in the air. Ah, me! This is an 'ard world!

(Don't take any notice of me, really. I still build castles

in the air because I can't help myself. It must be a sort of disease.)

By the way, before I forget, I intend to write to you every ten days or fortnight from now on. (Don't pass out, I really mean it.) I suppose, just because I am making a good resolution like that, you will move somewhere and won't get the letters. If you moved here I wouldn't mind, though, but there doesn't seem much hope.

I feel terribly guilty about not even cabling you for your birthday. I honestly meant to do so, but we were at sea at the time, and when we arrived here it was too late. By the way, how old are you? I know it's a rude question to ask a lady, but gentlemen don't mind telling their ages, do they? I hope you don't. Anyway, they say life begins at forty (cheery soul speaking). In that case, I don't exist yet. Actually, as time goes on, ages don't matter really.

I must tell you what happened the other night. Mummy and Daddy and I were having a walk after dinner when we saw someone in the street yelling frantically for a policeman. Of course, we dashed up and found it was Mrs (Pippy) Gardener. We asked her what the matter was and she told us that there was a man in a flat which hadn't been tenanted for months. She and Mr Gardiner thought it was a burglar and were afraid he would get into their flat. Anyway she took us up to the flat, and Daddy and Mr Gardiner banged on the door and shouted and made an awful din, but couldn't get any answer. Mummy, Mrs Gardiner and I hovered in the background.

After about five minutes they gave up, and then Mr Gardiner saw a light and went up to the window and peeped in. All they saw was a man asleep in bed! What an anticlimax! I expected to see at least four desperate men inside and all we saw was the poor harmless man who owned the flat sleeping in his own bed with the light on! Apparently he had just come back from a long holiday.

Anyway we all went and drowned our sorrows afterwards

and had a good old chin-wag about Singapore and all the people there. I wish we were back there, don't you? Remember when you used to come and see us on Thursdays and Sundays. The trouble was, you always came when I was going to bed and I was always in my pyjamas.

I'm afraid there is no room for any more. One day I will write a legible letter, but the only reason why it is so cramped is that I want to send it Air Mail. Hope you get it soon. Cheerio! Tons and tons of love from Molly.

xxxxxxxxxxxxxxxxxxxxxxxxxxx

P.S. Write back soon.

29.10.42

Dearest Steve,

I expect you will be surprised to hear from me again so soon, but I'm keeping my promise so I will fire away.

To begin with, Daddy received a letter from you (please note that I didn't) dated 4th October but not posted until the 13th. That's a very bad habit you have, you know. You carry letters around with you for ages and forget to post them. You must try and correct it, my boy, otherwise Aunty will be very cross and she won't write to you anymore. Now don't cry! It's all for your own good, and Aunty knows best!

(How old do you feel now? About six I should think!)

Well now my lecture is over, where was I? Oh, yes! Your letter arrived today and inside it was an air graph from Cheesy [*Muriel Cheeseman, a friend from school*] and a bill. The first was very popular and the last was not. I wonder why? Actually it was from that silly old doctor I had when I had that fever. All he did was tell me to say "Ah" and prescribed nothing to eat (the old starver!) and complete rest and quiet when I didn't want to rest and be quiet. He charged £10.50 for that.

Cheesy's air graph contained the best news I have had

for a very long time. I've passed my School Cert! (Swoon! That's what I nearly did when I read the air graph.) Isn't it absolutely marvellous? The papers got home alright after all, and I've actually passed. I should have been very surprised if I'd failed because I found the exam much easier than I had expected, and deep down I had a feeling that I must have passed. I don't know all the details yet, so if an official-looking document addressed to Miss M. Lambert arrives at Melbourne Avenue, you can open it if you like and read all the details. I really mean it because it will save me having to tell you them. I expect I've failed in maths, but who cares as long as I've passed the jolly old exam. Don't forget what I have just said, will you? You can open it and read it, if you're interested, but send it on quickly and DON'T keep it in your pocket for a month or so, or Aunty will take drastic measures when we meet again.

[*Molly didn't just do well, she achieved Grade 1, the top grade. And despite her concern about maths, she still managed to pass. Her results were as follows: English Language – A; English Literature – A; French – A; Geography – C; History – A; Hygiene & Physiology – C; Latin – C; Maths – C; Religious Knowledge – C.*]

Well, that's one piece of news broken gently, I hope. (I'm an expert at breaking things now, but I don't usually break them gently, as you know of old. I'm referring to things, not facts – cups, plates, etc., and Susie's vases that used to shake every time I approached the window. Are they still there?)

I forgot to mention Cheesy's results. If I've done half as well, I shall consider myself a brainy specimen. Out of eight possible passes, she got one credit A in English. She only failed in one thing – history. Her art papers weren't counted, but I daresay she would have got a Credit A if she had finished. She seems to be very happy in England and is going to college to be an architect. Lucky old hag! That's what I would have liked to do – go to college, but there's still hope if the war hurries up and finishes. Anyway, in the meantime, being a shorthand typist isn't bad, and I shall probably end up liking it so much that I shan't want to do anything else.

Now for the second piece of good news. The PC [*Police Commissioner*] has come back and he was quite decent about the permits and we had no trouble about them. Of course, we are all bucked to death. Daddy is like a new man and looks as though a ton-weight has been lifted from his shoulders, and Mummy looks the same. It is such a relief after all our worrying to be able to stay here and settle down for a while. I'd still rather be in England, but it's nice to be settled anywhere after the last six months of uncertainty.

We are at last able to make plans again, whereas before we were only living from day to day. I suppose you are doing the same at the moment. Still, perhaps by the time this letter reaches you, you will have heard something. It would be just too good to be true if you were sent here, wouldn't it? We have had two pleasant surprises. Can't you manage it so that we get a third one? There's one consolation about your moving, anyway. Wherever you go, you are bound to call here, and we can see you then.

Well, we have been here nearly three weeks now, and I have been working for a fortnight. Tomorrow I'm going to draw my first wages. Whoopee! They won't be very much because I haven't been working for a full month, but they will be an absolute fortune to me. I shan't know what to do with such a lot of money. Buy some clothes and things, I suppose, and save the rest. Next month I'm going to save one third, give a third to Mummy and Daddy and spend the rest on Xmas presents and things.

I shall be able to buy some lovely presents for people this year. It's a lovely feeling to think I shall be independent and not have to ask Mummy for money to buy a present for Daddy, and vice versa. (Sometimes they had to pay for their own presents!) I can send home some nice things now too without having to ask. Nice feeling, isn't it.

Every month I'm going to keep a list of things I buy and what they cost. Muriel Squibb does that. She's a worse Scrooge than I am! Daddy says I'll enjoy myself counting up my money every night, ironing out all the notes and putting them away in little bags! Isn't he an idiot? I think the permit business has gone to his head, but it's grand to see him acting the goat again. He's right back to his old form now. You know what an ass he can be when he likes (respectful child speaking of fond parent!).

All your letter to Daddy consisted of was a description of the sunsets you have been having there lately. I love watching the sun set, but if that's all that goes on there, I'd soon get tired of Colombo. How are Susie and Robbie? I have written to them from the boat. The shock will probably stun them.

Last week and the day before yesterday I played hockey for the Wrens against the crew of one of the ships in here. Phew! Was it rough, and did I get knocked around! After not playing for ten months and then playing in a mixed team, was pretty strenuous, I can tell you. Still, in spite of bumps and bruises and the most frightful stiffness in all my joints next day, I enjoyed it, although I played a most disgusting game. The Tonkin twins played as well. They are quite good sports. You'd never recognise them now. They have got awfully fat, but are still as pretty as ever.

Tons and tons of love from Molly xxxxxxxx

5th November 1942

Dearest Steve,

I just received a letter from you dated 26/10/42. Poor old thing! You do sound fed up with life! It must be rotten for you stuck in Colombo like you are when everyone else has gone. It can't last much longer. Do cheer up. I think you must have had a very bad attack of depression when you wrote that letter. It sounds horribly miserable.

This is the third letter in three weeks to make up for my not sending you a cable for your birthday. I do feel beastly about that, Steve, honestly. I could kick myself good and hard. All the kicking in the world won't repair the fact that it was simply horrible of me to neglect to send one. I know you think I forgot it – I can tell by the letter, but I really didn't.

The trouble was that on Oct 10th I was on the high seas, and when I arrived here I thought it would be too late to send one then. I do wish I had now, especially as you have been feeling so miserable.

Now, before I go any further, you are going to hear a few home truths, so look out. To begin with, you commenced your letter with 'Molly, my child'!!! Once and for all, will you realise I am sixteen-and-a-half, and feel lots older, even if I don't look it, and you are not my grandfather. Please address me on equal terms, or else I shall address you as 'Nunc' again. I'm not sure I shouldn't have started my letter like that just to pay you back. G-r-r-h!

Next you go on to say you would like a snap of me as you would like to keep track of my change in appearance or you will never know me when you see me again – in 1999 at the rate things are going on. Well! Even if you don't intend to see me until then, you've got a nasty shock coming to you. I won't wait all that time, and being an only child I'm used to getting my own way so you can't escape me.

The next cheerful thing you go on to say is that every time you pass a birthday it's brought home to you how ancient you are becoming. Piffle! Booh! And Fiddlesticks!! A mere babe in arms. Life only begins at forty, so you've got a very, very long way to go before you even start living. The trouble with you is that you let yourself get morbid and it's terribly bad for you. Try and forget yourself, go around and do things and get interested in them. I know it's all very well to talk. I was exactly the same in Durban, but it's awful to think of you being so miserable when we are so happy being all together. You have been waiting for news for a long time now, so you are bound to hear something shortly. After all, everything comes to an end, and as Daddy used to write to us, 'it's a long lane without a pub in it'. Perhaps that's not said in the best of circles, but it is certainly expressive.

We like it here very much, but there's just one rather big thing missing. Now don't get a swollen head! The other night we debated on the question of what was missing to complete the happiness of the Lambert family, and after it was put to the vote the committee were unanimous in their decision. Can you guess what it was? (Sorry to put you in the neuter gender – you being the missing 'it').

To continue with my lecture – you finish up your letter by saying 'write to me sometimes if you have time'!!!!!!!!! You deserve to be shot for that remark. It hurt a bit besides making me wild. You know jolly well that I'll always have time to write to you, Steve, so don't make any more funny remarks about it.

There! Now I feel better, having got all that off my chest. I know you were only feeling miserable when you wrote that letter, and I suppose you have a right to be, the way things are for you at the moment, but don't think I'm going to stop writing to you or anything like that.

Well, to change the subject, today I had the afternoon off and had a lovely time blowing all my money (well, not all, but quite a lot). I'm terribly thrilled with a frock I have just bought. It is an American one and the price is terrible really, but I had to have it. I'm afraid I'm growing into a frightfully extravagant person, but when I see something like this frock and it fits me and I'm crazy about it, I just have to have it.

Mummy and Daddy like it very much, and I think you would like it too. I feel woozy (to quote Yseult) in it! It is a Deanna Durbin frock and looks awfully smart. It's really a sort of sports frock to wear on the beach, but it's lovely. Here is a picture (don't laugh) of it. It is navy and red and white and has a little coatee [*jacket*] of red and white stripes, with a hood lined with navy blue to match the frock, attached. The frock wouldn't really be anything without the jacket and hood.

(Figure 8.1 Pen and Ink Drawing of Molly's Dress, 1942 can be viewed in the gallery section of the website: http://www.lambertnagle.com)

I'm going to have a snap taken in it and will send it to you as soon as poss.

At the moment, the frock is being altered as it was too big, but I don't think it will spoil it. It has a very low back and no sleeves, but as I shall always wear the coatee it doesn't matter. I'm dying to get it back, but I'll have to wait until tomorrow. It's not very often I see something like that, but when I do, I get the most terrific kick out of buying it. The last thing I bought like that was my green sun-suit with the sailor collar. Remember it? I wish I still had it, but I'm afraid it wouldn't fit now because I've grown (both ways).

Quite a lot of nice things happened yesterday. I had the afternoon off, then I went shopping, then I met Daddy and inveigled him into the shop with the above results (ha ha!). He really didn't mind paying, though. In fact, he wouldn't let me pay for it myself. The last nice thing was getting a letter from you (or at least it ought to have been, and was until I opened it).

I don't think there is much more news to tell you so I will stop now. I hope something will have happened by the time this letter reaches you. Cheerio!

Lots of love from Molly

xxxxxxxxxxxxxxxxxxxxxxxxxxxxxxxxxxxxxxxxxxxxxxx

Flat No 4
Raynor House
Mombasa
E. Africa

23rd November 1942

Dearest Steve,

I have just this minute (please note) received your letter dated 3rd November and was terribly pleased to receive it. I was beginning to wonder what had happened and had visions of your being on your way home, or something equally horrible. I heaved a sigh of relief when I saw the old Colombo stamp on the letter. The evil day hasn't come yet, or at least it hadn't then. I don't know if it has or not now.

I wish letters didn't take so long to get here because I look forward such a lot to getting letters from you. Every time I open one now I get cold shivers down my spine because I'm afraid it will say you are going home. Can't you possibly stay put? Daddy wishes you could! I can't put it more clearly, so you'll have to use the jolly old grey cells a bit. If you can't do that, try and go to SA or, better still, come here. England is such a long way away! I know it's awfully dog in the mangerish of me, but as I can't go home, I don't want anyone I like to go home either. Dreadful of me, isn't it!

I can see that my letter from the ship wasn't too popular. All the excuse I have is that I had a lot of distractions at the time and was very lazy.

Your letter sounds a trifle more cheerful than the last, although not by any stretch of the imagination could it be called a cheery letter. Still, I don't blame you, I only wish I could come and cheer you up or that something would happen to have the desired effect. All I can do is write, and letters seem such futile things. Still, I suppose they are better than nothing; they certainly are to me, anyway. I hope you have received the snap I sent you by now. It isn't a very good one, but I intend to have a better one taken and enclose it in my next letter. Cameras are very difficult things here. One has to have all sorts of permits to be able to use them.

[*The ban on photography was to ensure that none of the military buildings, particularly where the allied code-breakers worked were identified.*]

Actually I had one taken with the Tonkin twins the other day. So if it is any good I'll send it along in my next letter.

Talking of letters, I actually had an air graph from Yseult the other day.

[*This was the first time Molly had heard from her best friend Yseult since she left Singapore. Steve must have made a remark about Molly's many male acquaintances, as here she is, indignantly denying that they are boyfriends.*]

You seem to be under the impression that I have millions and thousands of boyfriends who all write to me. Honestly, I don't know why you think that. Just because I met two on ships. The one like you doesn't write to me – you don't start writing to people you have only known for about five days. At least I don't! The only one that writes is Richard, and that isn't very often. When I do get a letter, it's always very short and sweet. [*Richard Hughes, one of the twins Molly met on Westernland. 'The one like you' she is referring to may have been Lieutenant Parsons, a naval officer.*] Actually, compared with all the other girls here I am remarkably free from such encumbrances (boyfriends I mean). I've known so few, except the ones in Hong Kong, that I always feel shy and awkward with ones of my own age, or a bit older. I suppose it's silly, but I can't help it.

Mummy and Daddy say I'm at the 'awkward' age, but I thought I'd passed that in Singapore. I seem to be getting worse instead of better, though. Still, in Durban I had a fellow sufferer in Muriel Squibb. We both hate walking out by ourselves. I never know what to do with my hands, so now I always carry a handbag (formerly regarded with loathing in Singapore). If I didn't have it now, I don't know what I should do. Muriel and I both hate doing anything conspicuous. It was awful in Durban – we couldn't walk two yards in the street without being yelled and catcalled at. I don't know why I tell you all this – it must be awfully boring for you.

Before I forget, though, I must tell you something funny! At least I thought it was because it's the first time it has happened to me. There is a little Marine orderly who stands just outside our office and is always staring in and grinning. [*The FECB operation, codenamed Kilindini, was based out of town at a former school. There was an armed guard that stood outside twenty-four hours a day. Don and Ciss found this amusing, as they felt that all the guard did was draw attention to the place when it was supposed to be secret.*] He can't be more than eighteen, and doesn't look as old as me. I always have to get the office keys from him, and every time he gives them to me he blushes right up to his ears. He is really rather sweet.

Well, anyway, the other day, as I was leaving the office he stopped me and said, "Are you doing anything tonight?" Well, of course, if I'd had any experience of that sort of thing I should have replied that I was going out, but like an idiot I blurted out no. Which, of course, was quite true. That completely tore things because then he asked me to go to the pictures with him!

It was awful! I muttered some excuse that I'd never been out with anyone by myself, so he said, "Oh well, there's always a first time. What about tomorrow?" He couldn't take a hint, so in the end I had to say that I didn't think I'd be allowed to. It was awfully difficult not to hurt his feelings, but I didn't want to go a bit, and even if I had, I don't suppose for a moment Mummy and Daddy would have let me.

Someone else asked me out to a dance the other night and I didn't want to go. At least, I wanted to go, but I hate going with people by myself. I'd be embarrassed if I had to go with someone alone. I suppose I'll have to one day, but I'm putting it off as long as I can. It would be nice to go with a crowd and I'd love it, but not by myself. Anyway, I told Daddy to tell him I was too young, so it was OK. Getting Daddy to play the heavy father is a godsend. My trouble is that I always think too much of what other people are thinking when I do things, and this is such a small place that it's very easy to get talked about.

Anyway, tomorrow night I am going to a real dance with Mummy and Daddy and am looking forward to it very much. I do hope it will be nice. I'm going to wear my blue frock with my zircon bracelet to match it (it was a lovely present and is the exact colour of my frock. You always think of nice things and I believe you bought it to match my long frock), and my new silver shoes that cost the awful price of £2. I'm almost frightened to wear them! They are a lovely silver kid and very comfortable and smart. The heels aren't very high – just nice and comfortable for dancing in. I shall wear my white bows I expect. You will see from the snap that I do my hair differently now – in a pageboy with two straight sausages down each side (not real sausages! Wouldn't I look funny if they were?). I mean sausage curls.

Doesn't all this sound worldly and conceited! I feel like a dissipated woman of the world! Don't think I'm really getting like that, because I'm not. At least, I hope I'm not! It is nice to go out sometimes though, isn't it?

I'm so glad you had a good night out at the Galle Face, but you are a bad man not to dance! It's no good making the excuse that your shoes were too tight because it just doesn't cut any ice with me. See! Now I'm getting into one of my tough moods, so you'd better look out! I do wish you were coming with us tomorrow night, though. Do you know it's the first night I will have worn my long frock to go out in that you haven't been with us? It won't be the same without you. Can't you spirit yourself here even if it's just for one night?

Can you remember all the New Year's Eves we had in Singapore? I'm dreading the thought of this one. Dry up, Molly Lambert! You're getting sentimental and morbid when you should be cheering Steve up. I'm ashamed of you! Your morbidness is catching, I think, so I'll change the subject. I'll tell you all about the dance in my next letter. Please excuse this one being all about me.

I'm longing yet dreading to hear from you in case of the contents of your next letter, but perhaps we might all be agreeably surprised when you do get the Admiralty's decision (says she, trying to be optimistic). Well anyway, WRITE BACK SOON. Mummy and Daddy send their best love and mine goes without saying. Cheerio!

Heaps and heaps of love, etc. from Molly

xxxxxxxxxxxxxxxxxxxxxxxxxxxxxxxxxxxxxxxxxxxxx

Flat No 4.
Raynor House
Mombasa

2nd December '42

Sir,

I received your two most spiffingly long, newsy and cheerful letters a few days ago. I'm so sorry I haven't replied before, but I had lots of 'duty' letters to get off my chest. Well, anyway I've got them over now, so now I can concentrate on answering your lovely long letters properly.

Before I go any further, though, I must apologise for my writing because my hand is shaking like a jelly. Not from liquor as you suggested in your letter, but owing to the fact that I have been playing a rather strenuous game of hockey. As a matter of fact I have just come out of the bath and am sitting dressed in my usual fashion (you know, a la Dorothy Lamour (some hopes!)), cooling off before I change for dinner. This time of the day and during the lunch-hour are the only times I get for letter writing.

Stop Press. Daddy has just come in to show me his new bathing shorts. He is sticking his chest out and making me feel his muscles! He says it's 5/- a time for feeling them! Isn't he crazy! He has just remarked that they show off his 'form' very nicely and is parading in front of the mirror like a turkey-cock. You must think we have all gone crazy or decided to turn nudist, but I assure you we are quite decent (but only just). Daddy is frightfully proud of his shorts. They are blue and cost £1.

Things like that are terribly expensive here when you can get them, which isn't often. The only English shop is Whiteaway and Laidlaw's, and even that doesn't stock much. Still, there are plenty of Indian shops, and material and things like that are fairly easy to obtain. Food is about the hardest thing to get here, and fresh milk is about as rare as diamonds. Still, we don't do badly as we have all our meals at the Palace, but it would be a nightmare to have to keep house here and do the catering. Mummy doesn't intend to do that, and I don't blame her.

The most important piece of news in your letter was that you are leaving Colombo to go to our 'first port of call' [*Bombay*] when we left there. I don't know whether to be glad or sorry. Of course, it is nearer this place and letters will not take so long now, and it is much better for you than being stuck in Colombo feeling like one of the world's forgotten men. On the whole, I think I'm glad.

It should be awfully interesting work. It must be rather fun to be starting a new organisation, and it will be very nice to go somewhere fresh.

If you are living in the town you must go and visit a most marvellous café called 'Monginis'. It is in Church Cross or St George's Cross or Market Cross – or is it South Cross Street? My information is, as usual, as clear as mud, but most people in the town know where it is. When we went ashore there we had a sort of lunch in Monginis. It wasn't a proper lunch, just a snack, but boy oh boy do they make good ice creams and fruit drinks and cakes! After Colombo, where we couldn't get any ice cream, it was marvellous! Can you get any there now? We can't get any here, worse luck! I'm pining for some. When you get to your destination, send me a couple of ship-loads, will you?

Anyway, don't forget to visit Monginis, will you. I advise you to go there for tea. They have quite a good orchestra and their cakes are lovely (says piggy-wig always thinking about her tummy).

We are all terribly glad that you aren't going to the UK yet anyway. As you say, "While there's life, there's hope", and perhaps someone in your department will pop off somewhere and you can come here. I get jolly annoyed when I see all of them around the town. It's not their fault, I know, but it's irritating all the same. Poor things! I expect they all wish themselves elsewhere. It's a funny world!

I was very amused with your description of your department. So the advantages far outweigh the disadvantages, do they? Now, of course, if I were your stenographer I would quite agree with you on that point! (Get up and bow!) You don't seem to believe me yet when I tell you that I am an exceedingly prim and proper person when at work. I come in quietly (no rude remarks if you please, Mr Stephens!) and shut the door very gently and say "Good morning" politely with a proper smile showing a small amount of tooth (I reserve my usual beaming grin for other occasions). I then draw up a chair (taking great care not to scrape it along the floor) and commence to take down dictation. Funnily enough, the Captain's name is 'Steve' too! Can't get away from them, can I! One day I shall make an awful faux pas and address him by that name. Then I should probably get the boot!

Oh yes, I'm a changed girl now, alright! You'd never know me if you saw how quiet and decorous I am!

My conscience has just given me a very nasty prick for my last sentence. I must confess! Since being in our office, I have managed to upset two bottles of ink all over the typewriter cover and break a drawer by slamming it too hard! Still, that's not really bad for me! In another couple of years I might turn into a tolerably careful person.

I was very intrigued by your description of the tenth day of the tenth month of the tenth year of the twentieth century! Yes, it must have been a great day! I wish I had been there to see it, but unfortunately I was in God's pocket so I missed all the fun. I suppose firework displays were held all over the country and the fountains ran with wine (like they did at the Restoration), says she airing her knowledge. It was a pity you weren't old enough to enjoy it properly. I don't suppose there has been a day like it since, except of course the first day of the fifth month of the twenty-sixth year of the twentieth century, when yours truly made her appearance! (Modest, aren't we!).

Actually you are a year younger than I thought you were, but then I never know anyone's age. There's one thing, though. I wish I didn't look so infernally (nice word!) young. No one here believes me when I say I'm sixteen-and-a-half. They all think I'm about fourteen still. It's jolly inconvenient, I can tell you, because although I'm doing a stenographer's work, I'm not getting my full salary because they all think I'm too young! Still, I think Daddy is going to see about that soon.

It isn't the money so much as the principle of the thing that annoys me. People look at me so condescendingly when I say I'm working, and the other day someone had the cheek to say "Working? Well, whatever do you do?" just as though I was some sort of imbecile. Was I wild! I then informed them very cuttingly that I was the captain's secretary (can't you see me with my nose in the air?) and they looked a bit squashed.

I'm afraid I rather enjoy squashing people, having undergone the process so many times myself. I enjoy being the squasher and not the squashed. (Horrible little cat I'm turning into lately!) Still, I only squash people I don't like, so you needn't worry. (Not that you need to, because in a competition of that nature I have a strong suspicion that I would come off a pretty poor second!)

By the way, you remember your dear friend, Mr Hayer? Well, he got torpedoed on the way home and had to pull in an open boat for eighteen hours! I think that was pretty bad punishment even for him, don't you? I don't know him, so I feel rather sorry for him, but judging from your accounts of him, he deserved it. Incidentally, the Carvers had the same experience, but they are alright and are still going on home. Daphne managed to save a suitcase full of make-up, but they lost everything else. I feel jolly sorry for them because it's pretty rotten to go home like that after being abroad for four years, and I know they had bought a lot of winter clothing before they left here. The Grists were in the same party. Can you imagine them in a lifeboat holding hands? It's awful to laugh over a thing like that really, but the temptation is very strong, isn't it?

Yesterday I went Christmas shopping, or at least I tried to go Christmas shopping. I've had your Xmas present planned ever since I left Colombo, but like a fool, I waited till I arrived here to go and buy it, and of course I can't get it! Still, I've found something else that I don't think you have, and I hope you will like.

Life goes on in much the same way as usual, but I never get time to be bored. I played golf (laugh if you dare! Gr-r-r!!) with Daddy yesterday. You would have split your sides if you had seen me, kicking up clouds of dust, hitting trees and killing people all over the course! Judging from the account you once gave me, in a letter when I was at school, of a game you had at the Johore Golf Club, if you and I had a game of golf it would be a case of the blind leading the blind!

Don't forget to write back soon and tell me about the new place. Xmas will probably be a thing of the past when you get this, but anyway here's wishing you a very, very happy Xmas and New Year from us all. We shall think of you on New Year's Eve and wish you were with us. It won't be the same without you. Cheerio!

Tons and tons of love, from Molly.

xxxxxxxxxxxxxxxxxxxxxxxxxxxxxxxxxxxxxxxxx

CHAPTER 9
– TAKE A BOW, MR STEPHENS

In early 1943 Molly must have been sent back to work at Naval HQ in a civilian department, as by the sounds of her letters to Steve, she's now working in a less pressured but rather dull and bureaucratic office.

Flat No 4
Raynor House
Mombasa

19th Feb 1943

Darling Steve!

[*Molly makes a reference to Steve's letter of 4 February which amused her as he was trying to make light of the fact that he'd been ill.*]

I'm really awfully sorry that you have been ill, though. Poor old thing. Do cheer up. After all, things could be a lot worse. You can throw something at me if you like. (You're quite justified). There's nothing worse than to keep feeling utterly and completely fed up with everyone and everything, then to be told that things could be a lot worse and "Just imagine if such and such a thing happened to you", etc. etc., by a lot of smug people. Ugh!

[*Molly does her best to cheer Steve up, but goes on to complain about the heat.*] We're all nearly passing out. However, Daddy still has enough strength to totter over to the sideboard for a quick [*drink*], so while there's life, there's hope.

Thanks for the information about a certain shop, Monginis by name, situated in *Churchgate Street*, Bombay. [*Monginis is still a Mumbai institution.*] I do think you are beastly, rubbing it in about all the ice cream you can get in Bombay when you know jolly well we can't get much of it here. Bah!

By the way, I like the situation of your offices on the top floor of the Metro Cinema, but I must say, I think it is shockingly bad organisation on your part, not even being able to get free seats. You must be losing your grip. Now, if you had me as your stenographer then things would really get moving.

I'd like to tell you a lot more about the office etc. and my working companions, but it would only be crossed out [*by the naval censor*] so I'll have to wait until I see you. I quite like it, except for the fact that the person whom I have the misfortune to be in the same room with is a complete and utter pain in the neck!! His attractions are many and varied and I'll describe them all to you one day, but I think the one which most endears him to me is his cough. If he doesn't do something about it soon, I shall go completely mad. I mean it! I've dropped small hints, then larger ones, and then absolute bricks, but it's all to no avail because he's got a hide like a rhinoceros. I've offered him cough sweets by the dozen, recommended Owbridge's Lung Tonic, Friar's Balsam, Zubes, Allenbury's Throat Pastilles and every other patent medicine I can think of, but does it do any good? NO! He just goes on coughing. Ugh!

I shall do something desperate one of these days, such as bashing him on the head with my typewriter, so don't be surprised if you pick up the paper at breakfast, and over your eggs and bacon, or whatever you have, you read the headline: 'Foul Murder in Mombasa. Young English girl believed guilty. Trial today', or something to that effect. Believe me, that's what will happen if he doesn't look out!

Sunday 21st Feb

I am writing this in the morning, being lucky enough to have a whole day off – lovely thought! I had all sorts of ideas as to how I was going to spend the morning, but most of them (except for this letter) have been frustrated by the fact that all the electricity has been turned off. Mummy and I had good intentions of making some cakes (we have an electric stove in the flat) and I wanted to use my [*sewing*] machine, but there you are – 'the best laid schemes of mice and men, etc. etc.'

This afternoon Daddy and I are going on a picnic with the Leland family (also ex-Singapore-ites). Mrs Leland works in Daddy's office and I work in Mr Leland's office (actually next door, but I do a lot of work for him).

[*Molly writes about her friend Muriel Squibb in Durban, who now has a boyfriend, and her friend Flora who will be stuck in South Africa for the duration of the war.*]

Thanks once again for telling me about the pyjie [pyjama] episode. [*Steve's pyjamas came back from the menders with one leg sewn up*]. Why don't you come here? With my machine I could sew up both arms and legs in about two minutes. What a wasted opportunity! Anyway, I hope you are feeling better now. Mummy and Daddy send their love. Write back soon.

Very much love, Molly xxxxxx

Despite Molly's good intentions to write to Steve more frequently, her next letter isn't until mid-March.

11th March 1943

My dear Steve,

I hope the shock of receiving a letter from me won't be too much for you. By the way, before proceeding, how do you like my new pen? Daddy brought it back from Nairobi where he has been spending a week's leave (without us, too). He didn't want to go, but we made him because he needed a change after being in the heat for such a long time.

Which reminds me, you need one as well. Why don't you take some leave and go upcountry? Go to Poona! It would be a change and would get you out of the awful rut you appear to be getting into in Bombay. It doesn't sound good to me at all. You should try and get out of it, you know. I know it's all very well my saying that, but we're all getting quite concerned about you.

[*Molly goes on to tease Steve about his photography hobby, referring to his enlarger as junk, but as his last letter seemed unhappy, she contradicts herself, remarking that photography might make him more cheerful.*]

I feel awful having such a good time here when you are having such a miserable one in Bombay. I do wish you could come here. I know you'd love it. Everyone is so jolly. It's just like Singapore – or rather Hong Kong, because the Singy people weren't so jolly, really. We always preferred the atmosphere of HK. This place is terribly lively and there's always something doing.

First of all I must refer to your letter. I do appreciate it when you write such cheery letters, because I know it must be an awful effort. I'm duly squashed about the spelling error in my letter and now know how to spell mathematical (thank you, teacher!) I must also apologise for suggesting that you should come here and relieve Pippy Gardiner, whom I now know is a mere ACE [*Assistant Chief Engineer*]. I always thought he was a CE [*Chief Engineer – Steve's job title*], hence the suggestion.

Well, if you like, come and relieve Mr King. Then I'd come and be your stenog. How does that appeal to you? I don't think that's a very good suggestion really, though (the latter one, I mean). The combination would hardly be conducive to work, would it? (I'm quoting you, of course!)

By the way, speaking of Mr King, did you know that his wife is here in the Wrens [*Women's Royal Naval Service*] (a 2nd Officer, I believe), and they both live in the Manor Hotel? Lucky to have been able to work that, weren't they? I didn't know that until a week or two ago when I enquired who the Wren was that was always with Mr King. I was quite relieved when I heard she was his wife, because I like him and should have hated to think of him going around with someone else when his wife was at home. This may sound priggish, and I expect you think it is, but I can't help thinking like that.

We saw them at a concert given by one of the ship's companies here the other day. Actually, it was a revue called 'All over the Place', and I thought it was absolutely marvellous. There wasn't a gap anywhere and the whole thing was frightfully well done. There were some jolly good jokes and some terribly realistic girls in it. Actually, there wasn't a real girl in it at all. If you can imagine a whole lot of sailors (mostly big hefty ones) tripping around in little ballet skirts, you will realise just how funny it was. I nearly had convulsions! I wish you could have seen it. I know you would have enjoyed it. Remember when you took us to see 'The Great Nicola' the night the *Royal Oak* was sunk?

[*The Great Nicola was an illusionist. Steve had taken Molly to see him when they were in Singapore on Saturday 14 October, 1939. The Royal Oak, a Royal Navy battleship, was sunk by a torpedo fired from a U-boat off the Orkney Islands, Scotland. Out of 1,219 crew, 883 lost their lives. It was a devastating blow to British morale so early on in the war. On his way home to the US after Singapore, the performer himself had a lucky escape at sea. His ship hit a mine and it sank with all his props, although he was rescued.*]

That was three years ago now. It doesn't seem as long as that, does it? Remember when we always used to go to the cinema the night I had to go back to school? Remember when we used to sing in the car coming back from Singy, and the time you bumped your head and we lost the key and sang 'Rolling Home' and came back to our bungalow and had celery for tea? That was fun, wasn't it? I could go on in this way forever, but I mustn't because I don't want to depress you. It doesn't depress me to think of all the nice times we used to have, though. There's no reason why we shouldn't have lots more in the future. Anyway, things always seem better in retrospect, don't they?

Daddy is writing to you to answer a letter you sent him. He's just come back from leave and I think he had quite a good time. By the way, did I tell you I've just had a frightfully snappy slack-suit made? It's blue linen and the tailor has made it marvellously. It fits as though I've been pasted into it, but heaven knows what will happen if I get any fatter. Still, at the moment it's jolly decent. I'll send you a snap because we have actually managed to get a film in this benighted town.

Cheerio! Tons of love from Molly xxxxxx

Molly typed her next letter to Steve from her office, pretending to her colleagues that it was work.

13th March 1943

My dear Steve,

Well, I'm in the office with nothing to do for once, and as I have just received another letter from you, dated 1st March, I am seizing the opportunity to type you a letter. By the way, that bit about having nothing to do for once was pure swank to make you think that I am an over-worked person. I often type my letters when there is a slack half-hour. At one time I would have never dreamt of doing so, but now I have to take any opportunity I can get.

[*She goes on to apologise, as she knows it's rude to type personal letters.*]

Mooky [*Muriel*] Squibb and I always type our letters to each other. Last week she wrote to me, and said at the end, "The boss has gone to Maritzburg. Hence this letter!" I'm worse because I don't even wait for the boss to go away. I just sit and brazenly type. Of course, I have ways and means of camouflage, i.e. lots of papers around my desk (the letter I'm answering hidden underneath, of course). When I see anyone coming, I gaze down at them with a frown of concentration for some minutes, then raise my eyes to heaven and commence typing busily with all the appearances of a hard-working stenographer. Ha!

[*Molly is glad Steve has met up with colleagues in Bombay as she doesn't like to think of him being lonely. In her youthful enthusiasm she is a little tactless, breezily telling him that Mombasa is now full of people they both knew in Singapore.*]

Everyone knows everyone else like they used to in Singy (or on the base, at least), and I love going down the main street here because I know everyone I meet (or practically everyone).

There's always a lovely breeze blowing in from the sea which keeps the place cool. We have only had one really hot spell when everyone just sat and dripped like we used to in Singapore, and even then it wasn't as bad as Colombo. In May the really cool season begins when people are really glad of coats and woollies. I can't believe it will be as cool as that, but everyone assures me that it is quite true.

By the way, as a point of interest, who is this Mrs Worthington-Simpson whom you are always referring to in your letters? Tell me all about her in your next letter.

[Just as Steve liked to tease Molly about her 'numerous boyfriends', I can detect a hint of jealousy there as Molly wouldn't have liked the thought that Steve had a girlfriend.]

Daddy has written to you and, I expect, told you all about his holiday upcountry. You should have seen his face when he came back! It was like a lobster. Still, I think he enjoyed himself, and he actually put on a pound! He weighs the large amount of 9 stone 7lbs now, but he looks quite well, which is all that matters really.

[While the British people had been living with food shortages and rationing since the start of the war, it was only in 1943 that rationing was introduced to East Africa.]

In the hotels up there you can't have fish and meat in the same meal, and if you have soup you can't have cheese. If one is allowed to have only one principal course, which is all one needs really, it ought to be a [*decent*] sized one, not a piece of fish or meat the size of a threepenny bit as they give you in most hotels.

Actually, we do better than anyone else in Mombasa. We nearly always have eggs for breakfast now, although I'll never really like them. Tea is my favourite meal, and lunch. By the way, I went to the dentist yesterday and had two small fillings, much to my relief. I was expecting something much worse, not having had anything done to my teeth since June 1941. Now I can sit back for another year or six months without worrying about them.

Oh yes!! I tried some more cooking with the lady next door the other day. We attempted to make a chocolate sponge. The first one was awful. The second one wasn't too bad, but Mummy didn't think much of either of them. Mrs Buckley knows as much about cooking as I do, which isn't a lot as you know, so really, if we had made something decent it would have been pure fluke. I've definitely come to the conclusion that I've a hoodoo over me as far as cooking is concerned, because Mrs Buckley's cakes have all been successes, except the ones she and I made.

Still, perhaps cake-making isn't in my line. I may have hidden talent for making savouries, etc. I've never tried to find out, or not yet at least, but I must do so in case I've been wasting all my [*ability*] on cakes (laugh if you dare). The trouble with me when I start cooking is that I eat half the cake before it even goes into the oven. I think I like raw cake even better than cake when it is cooked.

I haven't been playing quite so much hockey lately, but I don't mind. I played last Wednesday and got rolled on, of all things! The person that fell on top of me was rather hefty. However, he picked me up, and after he'd made sure I was all in one piece, we proceeded with the game. One gets used to such things in mixed hockey, you know! I must be getting tough because I don't take any notice of knocks and bangs etc. now, although being fallen on was a new experience. However, I'm still here. Very much so, in fact…

Dash it! Here comes someone with some work. Can't these people realise that I mustn't be disturbed when writing to you? Oh well, I suppose I'll have to stop for the time being. Cheerio.

[*Molly had had to pull out her unfinished letter from the typewriter and had been unable to line it up again straight when she went back to it.*]

Well, here I am again, fifteen minutes later. It wasn't much, thank goodness, but now this page is all crooked.

[*This part of the letter was handwritten.*] Well, I couldn't finish this letter yesterday, and as I don't go to the office today and can't use the typewriter, I am finishing it now. Will write again soon. Cheerio!

Tons of love and xxs from Molly. xxxxxxxxxxxxxxxxxxxxxxx

26th March 1943

My dear Steve,

I may as well give up the unequal struggle of trying to

compete with you in letter writing. I have the distraction of a [*sewing*] machine and lots of material waiting to be made up, games of hockey, French and all the other things that go on here, e.g. dances (not so often now, though), concerts and picnics. Don't get the impression that I am leading a dissipated life here, though. I haven't yet reached the stage that I have threatened to reach, e.g. long cigarette holder, Eton crop, terrifically painted lips and face, and cocktail-glass-in-hand. I am still more or less the same and still get taken for much younger than I am, which gets more annoying every day. Daddy tries to console me by saying "Wait until you're forty and are mistaken for thirty," etc., but it's cold comfort now. Besides, I've no guarantee that when I'm forty I won't be mistaken for fifty, have I?

[*Molly goes on to tell Steve about family news. She had received a letter from her new aunt, Betty, recently married to her favourite uncle, Clarence.*]

She is only twenty-two and sounds awfully jolly. I think I shall have to forgive her because she wrote me such a nice letter and seems to like all the things I like and do all the things I do. So I think we'd get along awfully well. (By the way, Betty calls him [*Clarence*] 'Ron', much to my amusement!)

We have just heard now that Clarence has left England and are rather hoping he may come here, although it's not very likely. Poor old Betty is awfully miserable, and Granny and Grandpa are frightfully fed up because I think he's the favourite. I do hope he comes here because it would be marvellous to see someone from England belonging to our family. Mrs Best wrote to us from Durban and said that she sat down in a bus next to her own brother who had arrived from England!

Oh dear! This letter is pretty awful, isn't it? Although it's 10.30 I haven't woken up yet, in spite of having nine hours sleep, so until I come out of my coma, I think I'll stop and continue when I have woken up.

Same time next morning. Well, I have woken up this morning after nine-and-a-half hours sleep, during which I had the most potty dreams imaginable. I still dream every night like I used to at Cameron's. Remember the silly ones I used to have there?

By the way, your parcel arrived yesterday. Not yours to me, but mine to you. What I think of the Ceylon postal authorities is too bad to write down. I have put it in the old camphor wood chest and am saving it until I see you again, or know definitely what is going to happen to you.

We played hockey the other night, and instead of being knocked down myself, I actually knocked someone else down. Getting tough, you see. You should have seen the look of surprise on his face when he found himself sitting on the ground!

Tomorrow I am going on a picnic with a whole lot of people, including the twins. We are going out for the whole day and it should be quite good fun. We are going out to some beach, 'White Sands' I think it is called, in one of the NSO [*Naval Supply Office*] lorries, which will be rather fun because the road is frightfully bumpy. (You needn't laugh. The lorry hasn't got a roof on it like our car, so there's no danger of my bumping my head like you did.)

I wish we had a place like Beach Kandy here. The bathing here isn't as good as Colombo because the sea is too far away (from where we live, at least) to go swimming much. The best beaches are a good way out, and you must have a car or lorry or truck, or some sort of conveyance, to get to them. Every time we go for hockey we always go in a truck, but it's quite good fun. All the same, it isn't half as much fun as riding in the old 'Jitterbug' [*Steve's car*] used to be, in spite of all the nasty things I used to say about her in Singapore. (Now get up and bow!) Wonder where she is now, poor old thing.

I'd give anything to see her drive up to our flat one day

with her usual chug-chugging and screeching of brakes (provided she wasn't driving herself, of course). She'd be awfully useful for hockey too. Can't you arrange with General Tojo [*the Prime Minister of Japan*] to have her sent here, and then you could come too and be the driver to drive us all to hockey? Of course, the salary wouldn't be much to start with, but there are many openings for a young man of intelligence who is willing to work hard, as they say in all the advertisements. For further particulars, apply to the Wrens' Quarters, Mombasa and an interview will be arranged at the earliest opportunity.

Last night I went to a gramophone record concert. They're held regularly here, and I have been two or three times before. It's all very informal. We sit on the floor on rugs and cushions which we have to provide ourselves, and the only lighting is a few candles, but it's the right sort of atmosphere for listening to music and I always enjoy going to them. We heard two of Mozart's compositions, one of which I had heard before and one I hadn't, Bach's *Brandenburg Concerto*, and Beethoven's *Pastoral Symphony*, which I like very much. The whole concert took about two-and-a-half hours, but it didn't seem that long.

Mr King is a regular attendant. I see him there every time I go. It's rather surprising to see how many sailors and soldiers go to the concerts, but there are no other facilities for listening to decent music here, except the wireless which isn't very dependable, so I expect they leap at the opportunity.

One of the things I mean to do, when we settle down in some place or other for a reasonable length of time, is buy a gramophone and lots of my favourite records. Then I can play them when I feel like it and not have to depend on the wireless. Another of my pet ambitions is to have masses of books and a little study all of my own. It's rather fun planning things like that for after the war, even if they don't come off. I change my plans nearly every day, but it's fun having them.

By the way, one of my latest ambitions if we go back to Hong Kong after the war is to go home via the Trans-Siberian railway. I have heard such glorious tales of it from Mr Baines, who is in the same office as I am and has done it two or three times, that nothing will satisfy me now but to try it myself. Imagine, you can get from Kobe to London in fourteen days, and at about half the price that a sea journey would cost, besides the experience and the wonderful scenery you pass through and all the places you stop at. You have to take your own provisions, but as you are sitting in a train all day, you won't want much. All the Baines took were some tins of tongue, bully beef, etc., and tins of mandarin oranges and biscuits. Water is supplied at all the stops, and you can take as much of the 'stronger' beverages as you wish without being charged corkage. I ought to have put that first, I suppose!

I mean to travel all over Europe one day and then retire in my little cottage in the country. When I relate all these things to Daddy he looks at me enquiringly and politely asks where all the money for these ventures is coming from, which completely spoils things. Why do people have to be practical and spoil all your nice castles in the air? Anyway, I'm saving up quite a lot of money in the Post Office like a wise and sensible person should do, and as I shall soon be getting a rise on account of my rapidly advancing years, I shall be able to save a bit more. (That is unless I discover I need a new frock or pair of shoes, which I very often do, not to mention shorts, slacks, etc.) I'm afraid I'm growing into an extravagant person and I'll have to put a stop to it.

Anyway, one of the girls is getting married in May, and as I have been invited to the wedding I simply must have a new frock, and a pair of shoes to go with it, mustn't I? (Any excuse does.) Besides, everyone else is having new frocks, etc., for it, so honour demands that I should have a new one as well. It is in the process of being made now (by the tailor because the material is too good for my amateurish efforts). It is plain navy blue with white at the neck and sleeves to relieve it, and a bunch of white violets at the shoulder. I shall wear my white 'Salvation Army bonnet' as you so rudely nicknamed it in Colombo, and white shoes, and I suppose gloves. (N.B. I was rather living in hopes of being a bridesmaid as she is a Catholic, but there's nothing doing, worse luck.)

As usual, this letter has been all about me and now there's no space for any more about anyone else. I will now proceed to kick myself for being so selfish. Ouch! Well, you deserve it, Molly, so I've no sympathy with you.

Mummy and Daddy still have a bottle of Plymouth Gin waiting for you when you come.

Cheerio! Tons of love from Molly xxxxxxx

There is a gap of two months before Molly writes to Steve again.

25th May 1943

Dearest Steve,

I feel a lot better now that I have, at last, managed to find out where you are and what you are doing. To begin with, I'm terribly glad you had a such a good time while on your travels. It seems to have made all the difference to you. I can tell it by your letter. Let's hope you won't ever get back into that horrible little rut again, either in Bombay or the UK. Goodness knows how many ships you have travelled in now. You apparently only went on seven on your journey.

Daddy received your Air Mail letter card from Basra, which rather gave us the impression that you didn't go much on it out there. I was very, very surprised when I saw an Indian stamp on your letter today because I quite expected not to hear from you again until you had reached the UK. What we all expected, and hoped for very much, was that we might possibly see you en route, but of course that hope is dead now.

For the last month we have been expecting to see you turn up, and lately I've been doing the most ridiculous things in the street, e.g. clutching Daddy's arm and saying frantically, "Look, I'm sure that's Steve coming up the road" and getting frightfully worked up, only to find that the person in question is someone quite different and doesn't bear the slightest resemblance to you. Mummy has been saving up 'licker' once more, and we've all been on tenterhooks – so much so that I was terrified of missing you while I was away on holiday. I was quite certain that you would come when I was away. It would be just the sort of thing that would happen. However, it hasn't, so I was wrong.

There are two people in this place who look very much like that caricature of you and remind me of you every time I see them, which is quite often in a small place like this. Now Mr Baines has taken to smoking cigars with exactly the same smell as the ones you used to smoke, and sometimes I really can't stand it. One afternoon when I was feeling particularly fed up, not having heard any news of you for ages, I nearly told him to stop smoking your cigars, because one connects certain things with certain people. Silly of me, but then I still haven't grown out of my stupid dreams yet. I hope this will convince you further that I haven't changed as much as you seem to think, if at all. The only thing you are quite right about is my having a good time here. I do, and I like it here almost as much as Hong Kong, but it still lacks one thing to make it perfect!

I don't think I realised how much I looked forward to your letters until they stopped coming. I think I took them too much for granted before and I didn't bother to answer them as well as I might have done. One of the reasons was being interrupted such a lot – in the office and out of it.

Did I tell you that we have Trixie (Mrs Mitchell, with whom I do French) living with us now? In case I didn't, I'll be more explicit. Trixie's husband is a prisoner of war in Japan now. He was a civil engineer in Penang and she was a teacher before she got married, but you'd never think so because she isn't at all 'true to type'. We've all got ridiculously fond of her, and I know you'd like her very much, too. We like the same people as a rule, so I'm quite certain you'd like Trixie. She is very blonde with lovely blue eyes and one of those golden-brown skins that I so much envy, and is really very attractive, as you'd quite believe if you saw her and knew her.

Actually, as Daddy says, her chief charm is not her face, which isn't really as pretty as Mummy's, but her manner. To quote Daddy (who is one of her most fervent admirers; I tease him about it when Mummy isn't there), she 'combines beauty with brains and charm', so there you have it, in a nutshell. Of course, she has thousands (well about ten, anyway) of boyfriends and we don't see as much of her as we would like. Although on the surface she appears to be having a very good time, as several catty people here have said she only does it to make herself forget about Eric (her husband) as much as possible.

She's really amazingly plucky about it all and only gives us an occasional peep behind the scenes, but it's quite enough to convince us that she feels it very much and we all admire the way she is standing up to it. It must be pretty tough at times. As we share a room and spend a fair amount of time together, I see a lot of things that make me realise just how tough it is and what an effort it must be to keep cheerful at times.

It was rather bad last night. She'd been out all day with Hal (one of the boyfriends who is rather morose and nicknamed 'The Spaniel' by us on account of his dog-like devotion to Trixie). He had been more morose than usual, and that combined with some atrocity story, told by a stupid, tactless idiot whom I'd like to strangle, succeeded in thoroughly depressing her. The result was that she started to think about Eric, trying to imagine what he'd be like when she next saw him.

I made some rather feeble jokes about it and succeeded in making her laugh. If I'd been sympathetic I should have probably ended up weeping on her shoulder, which wouldn't have helped a lot. So I cracked my little jokes and had a private weep in bed afterwards when she couldn't hear me. I do feel most desperately sorry for her, but there's nothing anyone can do about it.

Well, I seem to have rambled from the point somewhat, but at least I've given you a pen portrait of Trixie, which is rather necessary as I'll probably be mentioning her in my letters now. If you know roughly what she is like, it will be much easier for you. I think I was saying that I hardly ever get time to settle down to letter writing these days since Trixie appeared on the scene. We seem to live in a continual whirl of people coming and going in this little flat of ours. Now, of course, we have all of Trixie's friends – most of whom we know, too – added to the list of our own, so the result is that the flat is hardly ever empty. I suppose one shouldn't complain, and I do enjoy meeting different people and having lots of friends – although no one like you – but it's hardly conducive to letter writing, particularly when the letters are rather important.

Don't imagine from all this that I have a trail of boyfriends all waiting to pounce on me, because there again you will be wrong, my dear Watson. I don't look on them in quite the same light as I did in Singapore. (You needn't say, "I told you so." I can just imagine you saying it when you read this!) Well, you're right in your predictions to a certain extent, but I haven't quite descended to the level of Eton-cropped sherry-drinking sophisticated, blasé female-with-a-long-cigarette-holder that you seem to imagine I shall end up being. I must say, I can't quite see how I justify that opinion, and I certainly don't intend to try. I don't think it's fair to get all these silly bees in your bonnet about me, you know. How would you like it if I got one about you? Wait until I think up a nice juicy one and tell you exactly what I imagine you're going to be like.

I must say, I'm frightfully impressed with the way in which you've managed to read and answer all my six letters in one. It's really awfully good. (Now, get up and bow!). Perhaps you'll tell me the secret of your success, Mr Stephens, and please, could I have your autograph?

I have been moved from NHQ [*Naval Headquarters*] and am now working at the same place as Daddy [*back in FECB*]. I have only been there two days, but like it very much better. I know most of the people there pretty well, and they all seem a much nicer bunch. In any case, even if the work wasn't better, the relief of not having to sit opposite my pet aversion all day long would be worth anything!

The poor lamb [*Don*] has been really sick for the last month. His eyes this time, and doesn't he crow over me now he really has something wrong with him. He always said how unsympathetic I was, but unlike you (I hope) he really meant it.

Mummy and Daddy send lots of love to you and wish you would come here so that we could all have a glorious binge. I think I really would get tight that night – or try, anyhow. Don't go home too soon because [*there's*] such a lot more I want to write to you about. Thanks once again for the lovely letter. You don't know how pleased I was to get it.

Cheerio for the time being.

Very, very much love from Molly xxxxxxxxxxxxxxxxxx

This was Molly's last letter from East Africa, as the naval HQ, the Eastern Fleet and the code-breaking unit were moved back to Colombo in Ceylon.

So what did the code-breakers achieve while they were in Mombasa? Some historians have argued that they were too far away from the theatre of war to achieve much, but Michael Smith in *The Emperor's Codes – Bletchley Park and the Breaking of Japan's Secret Ciphers* argues otherwise.

While Alan Turing and his team at Bletchley were working on Germany's Enigma code, and the Americans were working on the Japanese Purple cipher, in Mombasa they were trying to crack the Japanese JN40 code. JN40 was the method the Japanese used to communicate with their navy and a way of hiding the movements of their warships. And the Japanese had gone and added an additional number to their enciphered code, making it all the more difficult to unravel. However, just as human error led to the unravelling of Enigma, a similar slip-up on the part of the Japanese led to a major breakthrough in Mombasa in September 1942.

CHAPTER 10
– ON HIS MAJESTY'S SECRET SERVICE

There was a gap of four months before Molly wrote to Steve again. He was now back in England while the Eastern Fleet and the codes and cipher personnel had been sent back to Ceylon.

Like a postcard, an air graph could be read by anyone as it wasn't sealed in an envelope. It still had to be read by the official naval censor, as the following one was.

Air graph to:
NDE Stephens Esq
C/OCE-in-C Department
Admiralty
ENGLAND

YWCA
Slave Island
Colombo
Ceylon

15th September 1943

My dear Steve,

This is going to be a rather hurried air graph just to let you know that we are now back in Colombo again after all our wanderings! We seem to be going around in a circle, don't we?

We knew this was going to happen a long time ago, but of course haven't be allowed to say anything about it. We had a lovely trip over here, especially Daddy as believe it or not, the ship was packed with Wrens! Daddy's been having the time of his life; at least, he ought to have had. I should think he must be one of the most envied men in the world.

I'm afraid I've been shockingly lazy during the voyage and have done practically nothing but eat and sleep. But still, I think there's going to be plenty to do here by the look of things, and I feel tons better for the rest. I've actually put on five pounds too, much to everyone's relief, and am feeling right on form again.

I do hope you can read this as I am writing it in a terrific hurry. By the way, don't faint at the address on this. I'm being billeted at the YWCA temporarily. Mummy and Daddy don't know where they are living yet.

I'll write a more detailed letter when I've finished unpacking, etc. Mummy and Daddy send their love and say they'll write when they have time.

Cheerio for the present,
Lots of love,
Molly

Molly has left home, and in her hurry to send her air graph, she forgot to tell Steve the reason why. She writes to him two days later from her new lodgings.

YWCA Guest House
Union Place
Slave Island
Colombo

17th September 1943

My darling Steve,

I expect you've received my air graph telling you of our arrival in this place by now, so the address on the top of this letter won't be quite such a shock to you as it might otherwise have been. As it is, you'll probably raise your eyebrows when I tell you I'm living here on my own, for the time being at least.

I started writing this letter before dinner, but luckily for you, after having eaten a colossal meal of chicken and ice cream I feel much better and almost at peace with the world again, so this letter won't be as morbid as it might have been. I always think a good meal helps one in times of stress such as these! Actually, I'm making a lot of fuss about nothing. This place is very nice indeed, only rather quiet after the GOH [*Grand Oriental Hotel*] where Mummy and Daddy have been billeted.

This is my first night here on my own and I'm feeling just a teeny-weeny bit down in the dumps, having had rather a harassing day, dashing around the town in the morning and going to a rather chaotic office in the afternoon. We have all been given fairly reasonable lodgings this time anyway, although when I arrived here yesterday, complete with luggage on the doorstep, feeling (and probably looking) like a country cousin, I was told that there was no room for me and that they knew nothing about me! Still, I have experienced something similar before, so it wasn't too much of a shock.

Things are more or less straightened out now, there

having been a hitch made in my case because another girl had been given my room. She was quite willing to share it, although she couldn't really be anything else as it was my room, so now I am installed here until the middle of next month when I shall probably find myself out on my neck. Mummy and Daddy are very comfortable in the GOH as it is central and near the office, and they would be quite willing to stay there if it wasn't for the fact that they are having to pay R650 per month for both of them! [*Around £50 a month – or equivalent to £2000 today.*] It will be simply impossible for them to stay there permanently, so goodness knows what we shall do. It's the same old thing again: the accommodation question is just as bad as ever, and so is the transport. Things have improved very little since we left, except for the food, which seems to be good everywhere, especially in this place.

I expect you're still wondering why on earth I'm living here and how Daddy and Mummy ever consented to it. Actually it's all of my own choosing as we talked it over before we came here. Mummy and Daddy are quite agreeable, but I can't help feeling that they'll crow like mad if I say I'm not too keen on it (which at the moment is quite true), so I'm determined to stick it out and show them that I can be independent and look after myself. It has a great deal to recommend it, being spotlessly clean, cool, quite central, and possessing two tennis courts situated in beautiful grounds. (That sounds like an estate agent's advertisement, doesn't it?)

The only thing that seems strange to me at the moment is the quietness! After the ship and Mombasa it's just like a morgue. If the Tonkins weren't here as well, I don't think I could stick sitting down to meals with a crowd of staid old maids and dear old ladies who speak in whispers and look at you over the tops of their specs! (Don't you ever do that to me. I hate it.)

However, having the Tonks makes a difference, and we liven the place up a bit at meal times by purposely making as much noise as possible. It will be pretty grim when they go, though, but perhaps by that time I shall have grown into the atmosphere of the place and shan't regard it as anything extraordinary. You wait until I've been here a month, you won't know me. I shall be the model of what a good resident of a Young Women's Christian Association should be (ahem, ahem!).

Molly's new found independence isn't turning out as well as she had hoped and already she's feeling lonely. Here she is writing to Steve again just two days later.

19th September

Well, I'm afraid I succumbed to sleep the night before last, but I intend to finish this off tonight. Today is Sunday, but it's rather difficult to believe it because we have all been working. Things are still chaotic, but I daresay everything will improve in time. At the moment we are all pretty down in the dumps, and Mummy and Daddy and I have just been having a thoroughly good groan in the Tonks' room. Remember the lovely moans we all used to have here before? It seems quite like old times again, except that we miss you terribly.

Everywhere I go in this place brings back memories of the last time I lived here, especially when we saw Susie and Robbie again. They seemed quite pleased to see us and we had a long chat about the old days at 38 Melbourne Avenue, but I don't particularly want to go out there until I can get more used to the idea of Colombo without you in it. Hardly flattering to you to be connected to a hole like this, though, is it?

It honestly doesn't seem to have improved a scrap.

We are simply at our wits end to know what to do about accommodation, but luckily everyone else is having to face the same problem, so perhaps they [*Admiralty*] will do something about us. The Tonkins have to be out of here by the end of the month and have absolutely nowhere to go. Mummy and Daddy won't be able to afford the GOH for very long. The Townsends, Carvers, etc., etc. are all in the same position, and even all the 'big noises' in the office are grumbling about the amount of money they are losing.

I'm particularly badly off as I draw the large sum of R100/- per month, plus rather a doubtful subsistence of R70/- which may or may not come off.

[*Molly was being paid the local rate, and her pay and subsistence worked out, in today's money, at around £500 a month. As Don was having to pay four times that amount per month for their accommodation, no wonder he thought Molly was being exploited.*]

The reason for my colossal salary is simply that the powers that be here think that I haven't reached an advanced enough age to be paid a decent wage, even though I've been doing the work for nearly a year now! Bah! Oh well, I'll soon be eighteen, which I suppose is some consolation, although if I really had to live on my own, I should have the large sum of R55 per month for clothes, recreation and everything else! It doesn't really get me down very often because I'll never have anything to worry about while I have Mummy and Daddy.

Daddy's the one that makes the most fuss about it because he thinks it is so unfair. It's rather amusing at times, because he gets simply wild if I stay a minute longer than I have to in order to get some work finished for someone, who gets equally wild if I don't finish it! I'm afraid relations are often a bit strained between us on that point, although I can quite see his point of view. He's had a lot more experience of the people we work with than I have, and I'm afraid all this gets him down a bit at times.

Remember how bolshie you used to be when we were here before? I used to get horribly worried and think something terrible would happen to you, but I'm beginning to realise you were both quite justified. I'm afraid if I stay in this place for very long, I'm going to be as bad. Still, we've had some laughs since we arrived, and things aren't really as bad as we make them out to be. We always moan when we go to a new place until things are straightened out a little. I think we were pretty spoiled in Mombasa because we were very happy there and didn't want to leave it a bit.

I wonder what you'd say if you saw me now. I'm writing this after dinner on the verandah as it's cooler. In an adjoining room, four rather old ladies are knitting and the wireless is playing nice Sunday evening chamber music. You can hear a pin drop. This will get me down sooner or later. Luckily I'm too busy writing to you, or else I might be tempted to get up and scream, drop a few books, bang a few plates together, turn a few somersaults – do anything to make a bit of noise.

Wow, what a contrast to last night! We had such fun. Some of the engineers on the ship met Mummy yesterday evening with a tale of woe about not being able to get any girls to make up a party and asked us if we would come. After a lot of bother trying to find Mummy's and my evening frocks and Daddy's evening clothes, which he couldn't wear after all as he'd packed them in the camphor box, we managed to get ourselves ready. It only took us an hour-and-a-half, which is quite good for us. Of course, it was Daddy. He takes such a long time to get ready.

First of all, we had a simply marvellous dinner at the GOH, and then we went on to the Galle Face to dance. It's the first time I've ever been, although I'd often wanted to go when we were here before. There were crowds of people there and it was rather a squash, but it was great fun. We all enjoyed it, especially Daddy as he only had to dance once, and that was because I made him. It was an old-fashioned waltz, and I still think he does it better than anyone I've met yet.

[*The Galle Face Hotel was (and still is) the grandest hotel in Colombo.*]

We had great fun coming back in the taxi, but I'm afraid my reputation here will be gone forever now, as they [*presumably Don and Ciss and whoever else they shared a lift with*] would sing as the taxi drew up outside the gate. I practically had to go down on my knees to make them stop. I had to climb over the gate, too, as it was locked when we got back, but luckily no one saw me. After hanging around outside, trying to attract the attention of the night watchman, I managed to get in without waking the whole house up. Rather a wonder when I come to think of it, as I did one of my tripping up acts on the way in. Why must people put things where other people can fall over them? Still, there's hope for me yet. Perhaps living in the YWCA will cure me of my bad habits.

Next night:

Well, here I am again, back in my little bug hutch as Daddy calls my room. Tonight I have it to myself because the other girl's husband has arrived and they're both living in the GOH now. It's lovely because now I can sit down and write as much as I like without being disturbed. As usual I have just got home (at 7.30 to be exact) and only had time to bath and change before dinner. I wasn't actually working until 7.30, although Daddy was, but by the time we'd all ambled around the town and had long discussions which didn't go anywhere, it was time to come home. Really, I simply haven't had time to get morbid, which is just as well. Daddy and Mummy are pretty fed up with life, especially Daddy, but I'm not at the moment.

By the way, don't address your letters here, as I may not

be here by the time they arrive. Just address them as I told you in my last letter:

C/O COISEF [*Chief of Intelligence Staff Eastern Fleet*]
C/O GPO London

I really must stop now as there's simply piles of washing, ironing, and mending to do (sound like an old married woman with about ten children, don't I!). Such are the joys of living alone.

Do please hurry up and write because it seems ages since I heard from you.

Mummy and Daddy send their love. Cheerio for the present.

Tons of love from Molly.xxxxxxxxxxxx

Room 146
GOH
Colombo

1st October, 1943

My dear Steve,

Here is another change of address to puzzle you a little more. You can tell that my career as a member of the YWCA was pretty short-lived. I'm afraid I couldn't stick it, as it meant I never saw Mummy and Daddy after five in the evening, and it was really rather lonely.

Anyway, I'm installed in the GOH in a room of my own for the time being, until we can find something better (or perhaps I should say a little less expensive!). This hotel would be jolly nice if it wasn't for the burning money question. It's very lively (especially after the YW) and is certainly the best place to be in at the moment. As we are all in our usual depressed state, owing to the various problems we have to face every time we move to a new place, we're hoping to get a half share in a house later on.

I don't think there is any chance of our returning to 38 Melbourne Avenue, which is just as well because I'd simply hate it there now. It was quite bad enough going down there the other day when I called in to see Pat (you remember, she lived next door but one to us). Of course she was simply amazed when I rolled up on my bicycle and looked at me as if she thought I were a ghost. However, I assured her I was very much alive – which, after I'd talked solidly for about an hour, she was probably quite ready to believe.

To all outward appearances, Melbourne Avenue hasn't changed a bit since I left, but that's as far as it goes. Everything I ever connected it with has changed. It seems silly, I know, but I quite expected to see you come walking out of No 38. In fact, I still expect to see you when I pass familiar places here, [*even when I know*] that you're thousands of miles away in a much better place.

Things are very different for me now that I'm working instead of idling my time away as I was last time [*in early 1942 when Molly was fifteen.*] It certainly makes a lot of difference having a job of work to get on with. Nothing takes your mind off things better than that, and the time goes very quickly. There hasn't really been time to get a bad attack of the 'blues' yet. Tomorrow I shall be a lady of leisure, it's true, but I'm exploring the 'Pettah' [*a lively area of Colombo known for its markets and bazaars*] with Mummy in the morning, and going out to find out about French lessons at some convent with one of the Wrens in the afternoon, so that there won't be time to get depressed then, either.

We've met quite a number of old acquaintances since we have been here, including Mr Murray-Clarke, whom we certainly didn't expect to see so soon. Mr Murray-Clarke said I look a lot older, so that's a comfort. I think it's my new hair-style. ('Up' at the front and parted on the side, instead of the middle). Most people say it's a much-needed improvement to the jolly old viz (short for 'visage', a Lambert-Cheeseman expression). Which reminds me, I haven't heard from Cheesy [*Muriel Cheeseman*] for ages, although we've heard indirectly that Mrs C is First Officer in the Wrens. All my friends' mothers seem to patronise the Wrens. Yseult said her mother was joining up as well. The next thing I shall hear is that Mrs Squibb has joined the ranks. Then Mummy will have to.

[*Molly goes on to say that they were invited to a dance at the Civilian Officers Mess, where she met a mutual friend from the Singapore Naval Base.*]

He was a bit staggered to think that we still hadn't been home. Most people are now when we meet them again. The first remark they generally make is "What? Are you still out here?" or words to that effect! Still, we're pretty used to that by now. That's one thing, if you do come out again and we're still here, you'll know what not to say when you meet us, won't you?

Daddy was actually reduced to orange squash last night, so you can tell that things are pretty fierce when something like that happens. The last 'tot' of whisky passed away, surrounded by loving friends and relatives, on the evening of Friday, October 1st 1943. It's loss is mourned by all. (RIP!)

Stop Press: I'm writing this on Saturday night. At this moment I'm feeling absolutely fed up. I was sitting downstairs with Mummy and Daddy and Mr Murray-Clarke, listening to a band play dance music and simply itching to dance, and now I've gone to bed, everyone is dancing. I simply can't go back. Honestly, I do love dancing. The music is still playing, but as I haven't any cotton wool [*for her ears*], I'll just have to endure it I suppose.

I'd better stop for the time being because you might be shocked at my language. I'm in a BAD TEMPER, so I'll pipe down for the night.

The band has just played 'God Save the King', so now I feel a bit better (sour grapes). Goodnight!

I've just realised that it will be your birthday soon (today being the 5th), so before I forget, here's wishing you a very happy one.

Do write back soon and tell me how you like England.

Very much love from Molly xxxxxxx

Xxxxxxxxxxxxxxxxxxxxxxxxxxxxxxxxxxxxxxxxxxxxxxxxxx xxxxxxxxx

(Special for birthday) xxxxx

This next letter was written on hotel headed notepaper with a printed line drawing of an elephant.

Grand Oriental Hotel
Colombo
Ceylon

8th October 1943

My dear Steve,

I've just received your three air mail letter cards! They are the first letters of any kind I have had since coming here, so I am feeling very pleased with life at the moment.

Unfortunately we are only allowed to send [*air mail letter cards*] through the office, where they are censored by the person who sits at the next desk. If I didn't actually see the censoring being done in front of me, I wouldn't mind, but I don't particularly care to have all my correspondence read by someone with whom I am so much in contact. For the time being at least, I shall confine myself to airmail letters. I believe they are almost as fast now anyway.

You seem to have had a most unusual trip home. I thought our movements were complicated enough for anyone, but I'll have to give you points for yours now. I wonder when we shall stop. I get so sick of it sometimes. Every place we go to seems worse than the one before, although I suppose things will improve, as they always do. My main interest at the moment is my work. Without it I think things would be pretty rotten, but thank goodness I'm kept too busy to sit down and get morbid.

The main thing that gets me down here, as in Kilindini, is loneliness. There are very few girls of my own age, except the Wrens whom I like very much indeed. I am seriously thinking of joining. Perhaps I'm mad, but out here, anyway, the advantages of being in the service far outweigh the disadvantages. In my case, the main attraction is the companionship, and, to a certain extent, the good times that they all get, which I feel I ought to be getting and so far haven't had. I often think it would be a good thing to get away from everyone and start afresh, as it were, and if I joined something like the Wrens, I think I'd be treated more as a grown-up person than a child. Anyway, I'm not going to be in too much of a hurry to do anything about it yet. In any case I can't, as I had a talk the other day with the OC [*Chief Officer*] Wren and she told me that nothing had come through about being able to enrol new Wrens yet, although I think it won't be very long. I hope not, anyway, as the quicker I join up, the less time I shall have to do out here.

We honestly don't look like going home for ages yet, so I feel that while I'm here I might as well have all the fun I can get, and anyway it's an experience that will probably do me a lot of good. I'm sure I'm jolly spoiled, really, and I know I'm selfish and can't, or won't, see other people's points of view.

I've spent quite a lot of time at the Wrennery off and on in the past year, and although there are plenty of snags to it, mainly the loss of one's freedom and individuality, it reminds me so much of Cameron's where I was so happy.

I feel sure I'd love it, once I'd settled down. Of course Mummy and Daddy think I'm crazy, but they're naturally rather biased. Anyway, they say if I really want to they won't stop me, and it's too late to do anything about it once I've joined. Do write and tell me if you think I'm crazy. I'd like to have your opinion on it because it's rather a big step to take.

You still seem to be wondering about the fate of the bracelet. I'm terribly sorry, because I felt sure I'd told you in one of my letters of its safe arrival and how pleased I am with it. Anyway, I must thank you again for it because it really is a beauty. I wear it with all my evening dresses (well, both of them, anyway!) and even bought a little silver filigree butterfly brooch to go with it. When I want to be really grand I wear both with a dark frock, and simply wouldn't so much as glance at you if you happened to walk in when I was wearing them (much!). Well, of course, I might acknowledge you. After all, you did give me the bracelet!

I'm thrilled about the silver compact and can hardly wait until it arrives. You know, when you send such nice things, I feel a thoroughly spoiled and pampered young woman and could kick myself for ever even daring to grumble about anything. Mummy adds to it by saying she had to wait thirty-five years before she got a silver compact (the Siamese silver one Daddy gave her one Xmas in Singapore). It will be most useful too. You're quite right, I do powder my nose now. So would you if yours shone like mine does! What a lovely thought: I shall think of you every time I do it, and as that's pretty often, you'll be a much thought-of person!

We are still in the GOH, as you've probably noticed, but will have to look around for something else ere long or we shall all be in the workhouse.

How do you like Bath? You're very naughty and never venture any opinions on the places you go to. It must have been lovely going back to Southampton and seeing your people and all your friends. Is it very much changed? I suppose you'll try and get moved there now, won't you.

I was interested to hear about Cheesy. Do give her my love when you see her and tell her to write to a 'poor exile' when she has a moment to spare. I expect she's kept pretty busy at the university. I still envy her and Pam and Macky being able to carry on schooling, but I feel it's too late for me to do that now, so joining the Wrens is the next best thing. As I am at present, I feel I am missing things both ways.

From all accounts, England seems a pretty good place to be out of at the moment, and now that the possibility of some sort of career is pretty remote, I'd far rather be here, except for wanting to see you and a few others again. What would be the best thing is for you to come out here again, but I don't suppose that appeals to you much.

[*It must have been very frustrating for Molly as she'd done better at School Certificate than her friends, but they had gone on to university as they had been able to finish school in England.*]

By the way, you'll be glad to hear that I've taken your lecture to heart. Actually, I've put on four lbs, and by the amount I eat now I ought to make up my lost stone. Another thing I've taken to heart is the lecture on 'taking my likker'. I'll have to have more practice, won't I! I wasn't really surprised to hear about the girls in England nowadays as most of the Wrens can do their share. Anyway, times are changing and war does funny things to people.

I think it's best if you still continue to use the office address as we don't know exactly what our movements will be. We may continue to live in this hotel, I may soon be an inhabitant of the Wrennery, or we may move to some other hotel or house. Anyway, for the present, address your letters to:

M. Lambert
C/O COIS
Naval Headquarters
Colombo

I hope you can read this awful writing, but nowadays I never have time to do any typing in the office.

Once again, here's wishing you a very happy birthday. Do write back soon. Cheerio!

Tons of love from Molly xxxxxxx

P.S. Mummy and Daddy send their love

[October 1943 is where the bundle of wartime letters in the family archive come to an end.]

Molly decided against becoming a Wren as she was told she would have to serve a minimum three year term out in the Far East before being allowed home to England. In September 1944 she found out that she had been granted an exemption from Matriculation, the advanced qualification she needed on top of School Certificate to get into higher education. For a girl with ambition, this was a defining moment: no longer was she forced to settle for second best.

PART 2
1945–1967

CHAPTER 11
– NURSE LAMBERT

In December 1944, Molly, now a young woman of eighteen, stepped onto English soil for the first time in seven years. With Ciss and Don still in Ceylon, she stayed with Don's mother at 5 Cornwall Street, Shepton Mallett, Somerset. The following year, in April Molly moved 18 miles away to Bath, working again for the Admiralty as a stenographer and living at 33 Pulteney Street in the Women's Royal Navy Service hostel. Steve was based at the same Admiralty office, and Molly told me he would treat her to meals out to supplement the institutional food served at the hostel.

Don was granted six weeks paid leave in England in May 1945. By then he'd been promoted to Assistant Secretary to Chief of Intelligence Staff, East India, a rank that entitled him and Ciss to travel by plane. It had been four years since Steve, Molly, Don and Ciss had met up together. What a reunion that must have been.

After the celebrations, Don's first task was to try to secure Molly's future. Molly had settled on nursing as a career, but soon found that if she wanted to train at a top London teaching hospital there were a few hurdles to overcome. She was desperate to wear the dashing red sash and blue cape of St Thomas's, the hospital where Cecilia Tallis (the character played by Keira Knightley in the film *Atonement*) nursed. Unlike Cecilia, however, Molly didn't come from an influential family so St Thomas's turned her down.

Next on her list was Guy's. One of London's oldest teaching hospitals, Guy's was founded by Sir Thomas Guy in 1725 to treat the poor and sick of Southwark. As there was a danger Guy's might not accept her either, Don asked his superiors at Admiralty House if they would have a 'quiet word' on Molly's behalf.

Don and Ciss had to return to Ceylon in July, where they remained until Japan formally surrendered in September. Meanwhile, Molly was still working in Bath, but she did manage to secure an interview with Guy's. She made a good impression with the interview panel and got in on her own merits. According to the Guy's Hospital register of applicants in a note dated 6 November 1945, she was considered a 'nice girl and suitable candidate'.

When Molly joined the Preliminary Training School on 20 February 1946 she was a year older than her peers. She entered the wards four months later on 13 June and was assigned to Mary, a female medical ward, for five weeks. Four months later on 12 October 1946, Molly signed her official contract with Guy's. Not only had she survived her probationary training, she was a step closer to a nursing qualification.

In later life, she recalled how she and her fellow students spent most of their basic training scared out of their wits. They were disciplined like military recruits, and at times Molly thought that she may as well have joined the Wrens.

(Figure 11.1 Molly in Guy's Uniform, 1946 can be viewed in the gallery section of the website: http://www.lambertnagle.com)

In an era before nursing assistants, once the trainees went on the wards they had to do all manner of menial tasks. Molly dreaded cleaning out the bedpans in the sluice room. She told me how raw and sore her hands became after hours of scrubbing with disinfectant. They had no protective gloves, and one of the occupational hazards for nurses was the risk of infection. In December 1946 Molly caught scabies from one of her patients and had to take sick leave.

She was astonished by how physically demanding the job was: she had to lift men twice her size and turn them over to prevent bedsores. But no matter whether she was emptying a bed-pan or laying out a dead body, a Guy's nurse still had to make sure that she looked presentable and that her uniform was clean. The starched hat Molly wore was held together by a complicated arrangement of stiff strings which were tied under the chin in a particular way. She ran the risk of quite literally tying herself in knots if she wasn't careful. Nurses were awarded their 'strings' as a rite of passage after a year as a Staff Nurse. Molly wore her Guy's uniform with pride. She'd fought hard to get in.

On 25 February 1947, a year after she had started basic training, she was assigned to the York Clinic, the psychiatric ward, for six weeks. After that, it was back to class to attend First Year School for five weeks. In May, she was sent to the gynaecological ward at Orpington in Kent for three months.

One of the major drawbacks to working in hospitals was shift work, especially night duty. Molly found it very difficult to stay awake at night and then sleep in the daytime at the nursing home as it was very noisy. Out of desperation, in order to get some decent sleep she started taking sleeping tablets. It would have begun innocently enough – perhaps one of her colleagues suggested she give them a try.

A former nurse who trained in the hospital system in the 1970s told me that the drugs trolley was the only 'perk' of many a weary nurse on night-duty, desperate to stay awake. They could help themselves to whatever they wanted and nobody would be any the wiser. Strict controls on access to the drugs cupboard in hospitals came much later.

Molly was twenty-one and working night shifts in her second year when she was promoted to Staff Nurse. Here she is writing to Steve in Bath, describing New Year's Eve in 1947.

HAPPY NEW YEAR!
The Nurses Home
Guy's Hospital
London S.E.1.

1st January 1948

My dear Steve,

Thank you very much for your two letters. I was so staggered when the second one arrived yesterday that I am replying straight away.

It's New Year's Eve, and we have just seen the New Year in with half a medicine glass of sherry and a biscuit. Not enough to be merry on, but better than nothing! Also, one of the patients who went out for the evening came in just before midnight, and as he is very dark, we had the traditional dark man as well. [*First footing is a tradition where a dark-haired man should be the first person over the threshold to bring good luck for the coming year.*]

Do you remember when you used to come to our house [*in Singapore*] on New Year's Eve? [*1941*] I can still see you now, coming up the steps to No 3 with a tin hat on. [*Steve was an air raid warden, and wardens all wore a tin hat with the letter W stamped on them.*] We'd been expecting an [*air*]raid that night and I'd gone to bed early, but I got up again and we all sat round being happily morbid. I can never remember whether it was the dry dock or the floating dock that we thought had been hit.

Incidentally, the dark patient has returned once again to change into his dinner jacket. He is then going out to do a round of London's night clubs. Luckily he isn't coming back here tonight. [*The first footer would undo all that good luck if he came back into the house.*]

We had the wireless on very softly and heard Robert Donat speaking [*British film actor of the 1940s and star of The 39 Steps*], and there was quite a lot of singing outside. I seem to have spent from midnight to one o'clock going around putting pieces of paper in all the doors, which have been rattling such a lot tonight.

I'm glad you like the pipe-cleaner and hope it will be of some use. Your present hasn't arrived yet and I'm getting rather worried, because the present you sent me for my last birthday never arrived either. I meant to tell you about it when we were in Plymouth because I wanted to know what it was, but I forgot. It will be very queer if this is lost as well. There is a Sister Lambert here and her initials are M E, but I'm sure she wouldn't have had both parcels without saying something. I have never had any other parcels go astray while I have been at Guy's.

Did you have a nice Christmas? We had a very nice time at Plymouth, but the journey down on Christmas Day was pretty grim. I left Paddington at 10.30 and didn't get to Plymouth till 6.15. We went via Bath and Bristol, and I should think we stopped at every station on the way. Luckily I had a thermos of tea with me, because there wasn't a thing to be had at any of the stations, though there would have been plenty of time to eat a meal at every station judging by the length of time we stayed at each one. The only good thing about the journey was that I had nice travelling companions – an elderly-looking lady and her little girl. The elderly lady had been abroad – in fact, all over the world – so she was very interesting to talk to, and the little girl was rather sweet.

Yseult and Sam were also in Plymouth and I went around to see them twice while I was there. We had a very quiet time, really, but it was quite pleasant and made a break from Christmas in hospital, even though that is good fun. [*Molly's friend Yseult, whom she had known from childhood, died a tragically early death not long after from leukaemia. Back then the survival rate for the disease was poor. Yseult lived on in Molly's memory and in photographs, and Molly talked about her with affection and warmth.*]

On the way back, I got into the same carriage as a girl I knew in Colombo. Her name was Armanel Wilcox, now Jones, and she has a sweet little boy. There were two children in the carriage, and they kept us all in fits. Roger (Armanel's little boy) kept putting her hat on – he looked so funny.

I will stop now as I feel so sleepy that I must have forty winks – the senior pro is going to stay awake for me. I only have one more night on night duty and then I go into 'block' at Earl's Court. At least, we live out there and come into Guy's every day for lectures and classes. It is pretty grim at the moment according to some of my friends, but it's only for a fortnight.

I am at present in the throes of packing and am faced with the everlasting problem of how to get far more into my trunk and suitcases than they will hold. I think I shall be grey before I have finished!

See you when you come to London.

Lots of love, Molly

PS A happy New Year to you.

On 12 January 1948 it was back to class for Second Year School. The nurses did another six-week block of theory where they were taught gynaecology and obstetrics, medicine and an introduction to psychiatry. Molly wasn't the least bit squeamish and found the medical and surgical aspects of her training fascinating. She loved the drama of the operating theatre, even if it was assisting at something visceral or an orthopaedic operation involving an amputation. After that she went on rotation between Lydia (female surgical ward) and Luke (male surgical), followed by two weeks in Outpatients.

On 28 September, Molly went back to the psychiatric unit, York Clinic, for three months. She recalled having to assist in theatre, giving a patient an anaesthetic prior to ECT (Electro Convulsive Therapy). She tried to reassure me that at Guy's all patients were given general anaesthetics first, and I admired her bravery, knowing I could never have done half the things she had to do.

As noted in her nursing records, Molly was given her 'strings' on 6 November 1948.

Of course, life wasn't all work. Molly was surrounded by other young people and she enjoyed the camaraderie on and off duty. She and her friends made the most of their precious free time. Molly told me that in the late 1940s this part of Southwark (now the 'London Bridge Quarter' and dominated by the towering glass skyscraper, The Shard) was grimy and polluted from coal fires. There were gaping holes where houses once stood in the bomb-damaged streets, so whenever they could, Molly and her friends would escape the city for the countryside.

Molly found it hard to live in such a deprived area, and it was a shock for her to see so many malnourished children. In July 1948, her last year of training, the National Health Service, the British system of free universal health care, was introduced, and she was proud to be one of the first nurses to work for it. Guy's and the other big London hospitals had been set up in these deprived areas of London by philanthropists to treat the poor. Children and infants suffered the most, dying in their thousands from conditions like TB and diphtheria, but once the NHS had set up immunisation programmes, mortality rates dropped dramatically.

All of this was a world away from Molly's privileged life in the tropics. She missed playing sport, especially tennis and hockey, and the lack of exercise must have been a factor that contributed to her weight gain. Molly said she was at her fattest at Guy's because of all the starchy food, and once she weighed ten stone. That would have been difficult for her to carry off as she was only just over five feet tall, but stodgy food must have been a comfort during the bitterly cold winters of 1946 and 1947. From late January until mid-March 1947 Britain was in the grip of the coldest winter of the twentieth century, and despite the freezing conditions, coal for domestic consumers was rationed. There were restrictions on gas use and frequent power cuts.

Maureen Kermode, who was a young child at the time, recalls:

…my mother lighting the oven for warmth in the morning and opening its door to hang my vest over before I got dressed! The wonderful frost patterns on the bedroom windows and the icy linoleum against bare feet.

Food in restaurants was only marginally better than in the staff canteen as rationing was still in force. When Steve came up to London, he'd take Molly out for a meal. One time she ordered steak in a restaurant, but it didn't taste like any beef she'd ever eaten before and she was convinced it was horsemeat.

At the end of her third year in 1948, Molly returned to the nursing school for her last two weeks of block training. There were class discussions, practicals, tutorials and the last chance for her to ask the questions she needed clarifying before she took the Final State Exams. Once her final stage of training was over, after three years and nine weeks, Molly and her fellow nurses were left to revise.

It was a nerve-wracking time. Any gaps in the trainees' knowledge and experience would be apparent as they were tested in both practice and theory. Molly had given up her dream of going to university in exchange for a vocation, so for her failure wasn't an option. She crammed in as much revision as she could. She'd always done very well in exams at school, but school days were a long way behind her now. She hoped her photographic memory wouldn't fail her.

Molly passed her exams and received her registration certificate in March 1949. Like any medical registration, it had to be regularly renewed to ensure that the nurse was still fit to practise. Molly's last Practising Certificate, as a General and Obstetric midwife, was dated 21 January 1991 and was valid up until 20 January 1992.

After qualifying as an SRN (State Registered Nurse) in February 1949, Molly did a year's further training to become a sister. She was assigned to Bright, the female medical ward, then to two male surgical wards. After spending seven weeks working in the operating theatre in the surgical block, she was sent to Pembury in Kent in November 1949. She was there for three months, working on the deep X-ray wards where radiotherapy for cancer treatment was carried out. On completion of training on 1 March 1950, she left Guy's.

Of all the areas of nursing care, Molly felt that she could really make a difference in obstetrics. The miracle of birth never ceased to amaze her. However, just as newborn life instilled a sense of hope, there was a darker side to midwifery that involved comforting the heartbroken parents of babies stillborn or too premature to live more than a few days. But as the joy of birth outweighed the sorrow, Molly decided she wanted to specialise in midwifery, and after she received her nursing qualification she enrolled for further training.

Midwifery training took Molly to hospitals around the country. She completed the first stage of the two-part course in 1950, and after that took a midwifery job up in Cheshire. While there she met Fred Sherman, a clergyman's son from Meols. Molly became fond of Fred, and it wasn't long before he asked her to marry him.

The major snag was that Molly would have to renounce her Catholicism and become an Anglican. Molly accepted Fred's proposal, but wanted to discuss it with her parents. They were now back working in Singapore, and she accepted a six-month contract as a midwife with one of the large hospitals in Singapore so that she could spend time with them.

According to official passenger records, on 14 April 1951 Molly left England bound for Singapore on the P&O ship *Chusan*, officially engaged and looking forward to planning her wedding to Fred.

CHAPTER 12
– THE EMERGENCY

After six months in Singapore, and with her parents' blessing to marry Fred, Molly stepped aboard the SS *Chusan* once again. Travelling back to England with her friend Marjorie, she found two young rubber planters, Ian Ripley and his best friend Ian Stevenson (Malayan Steve), to be lively company. The two Ians were hoping to meet the right girls back home as it had been lonely working on a remote rubber estate in Malaya, but even in England it was going to be a challenge to find that special someone who was willing to start a new life abroad. If homesickness didn't get to her, the heat would, but if the Ians had no luck on this trip, it would be another three years before their next home leave.

At twenty-five, Ian Ripley was longing to settle down. However, only a brave woman would risk travelling to Malaya at that time. The country was in the grip of a guerrilla war, known as the Emergency. (Had it been called a civil war, the insurers, Lloyds of London, would never have paid compensation to the owners of the rubber estates and tin mines.) The epicentre of the conflict was in the rubber estates of Perak, where Ian Ripley went to work every day knowing that he might not come home. His was one of the loneliest and most dangerous jobs in the world at that time, as Chinese Malayan communist guerrillas were picking off and killing British planters.

In the Second World War the ethnically Chinese Malayan Communists and the British had in fact fought on the same side against their mutual enemy, Japan. The leader of the armed wing of the Malayan Chinese Communists, Chin Peng, enabled the Chinese guerrillas and the British Military Commando Force 136 to co-ordinate their attacks on the Japanese from their secret jungle camps. Chin Peng was even awarded an OBE for his bravery.

But post war, the uneasy relationship between Britain and the Chinese Malayan Communists unravelled. An avid anti-colonialist, Chin Peng tried to bring his grass-roots politics to the estate workers and encourage them to rise up and overthrow their British employers. Chin Peng's medal was rescinded by the British Government and he became the most hunted man in Asia.

A state of emergency was declared in June 1948 after three rubber planters were murdered in cold blood, and in August of that year, British troops arrived in the colony to try to counter the insurgency. Chin Peng, though, always denied ordering the murders of the three planters, blaming an undisciplined splinter group. The Malayan National Liberation Army, the armed wing of the Malayan Communist Party, had begun to attack rubber estates, tin mines, police stations and the transport system, and even went so far as to derail a train.

As the old, and some not so old, Malayan hands were slaughtered one by one, the rubber and tin mining companies had to advertise for their replacements in the British press. Ian Ripley answered the call, undeterred by the threat of danger. A wireless operator (chief petty officer) in the Fleet Air Arm, he had served on HMS *Venerable* in the Pacific Fleet during the Second World War until he was demobbed in 1947, and in that time he'd grown to love the Far East.

After the war, Ian trained in horticulture, working in the

apple orchards of Kent. Before he could leave for Malaya, he had to learn how to grow rubber and was sent on a crash course at Kew Gardens. Barely six months after those first murders on 16 June 1948, the newly promoted assistant manager left for the danger zone.

The price of rubber was high and the companies paid their managers well. Given the threats of intimidation, violence and hatred, you have to wonder why anyone would willingly volunteer to put themselves at risk the way that Ian did, but it was much more than a job to him. It was a way of life that he'd grown to love.

It wasn't just planters that were killed: sometimes their families were killed too. One particular murder caused revulsion throughout the country, and rather than raise sympathy for the terrorists, it merely hardened attitudes against them.

In November 1950, Susan Thomson, a British toddler, was in the care of her Malay ayah (nanny) when they were ambushed on the road up to the estate house. At the time her parents were at a funeral for another murdered planter. In the vehicle were the ayah's two children along with the Malay driver and house servant. The driver was killed instantly in the hail of bullets, and the servant critically injured. When the vehicle crashed to a stop, the gunmen spotted the British child and shot her in the head in front of the terrified ayah and her children. The irony was that that there had been no racial divide amongst these children. They had been inseparable companions and had loved each other like family.

In October 1951 the communists scored their greatest triumph of the entire Emergency. On 6 October, the guerrillas ambushed and murdered the British High Commissioner, Sir Henry Gurney, on the lonely road up to Cameron Highlands.

That autumn, Ian Ripley and Malayan Steve boarded

the SS *Chusan* in Penang for their first home leave in three years. As their jobs were fraught with danger, they intended to make the most of every moment, and it wasn't long before they had made up a foursome with Molly and Marjorie. Molly, who was engaged to Fred, encouraged Marjorie to get to know Ian, but he had other ideas.

He confided in Molly about his love life and found her to be a sympathetic listener, and as the voyage to England lasted three weeks, there were numerous opportunities for these cosy chats. After dinner, the foursome would stroll around the deck, but soon Molly and Ian paired off. Looking at the night sky with a girl by his side, emboldened by her encouraging responses, Ian seized the moment. He broached a new problem: he had found the right girl, only she was engaged to another man.

Molly, in turn, began to confide in Ian. Yes, she thought she was in love, but as Fred was the son of an Anglican vicar she would be the one who would have to convert. She told Ian that one of the reasons she'd left England and gone out to nurse in Singapore was to see if she could find a way to resolve the matter. Ciss and Don hadn't been keen on Molly giving up her Catholicism either, but they'd come round to it.

As Molly listened to Ian's tales of Malaya, she couldn't help but compare them to life in Meols. Ian, who was also Anglican, took his chances and told her that if he fell in love with a Catholic girl, he would be happy to convert so that they could marry. Molly was swept away by her shipboard suitor, and when he proposed, she immediately said yes. Intoxicated by love, Ian drank champagne out of Molly's shoe. It was the happiest moment of his life.

Banir Estate, Tapah, where Molly and Ian would be living was around 30 miles from Cameron Highlands, where Molly had gone to school. She was apprehensive but undeterred by the prospect of a guerrilla war right on their doorstep. If it really did get too dangerous on the estate, she could always escape to her parents in Singapore.

When their ship docked in England, the first thing Molly had to do was to travel up to Cheshire and break off her engagement to Fred. She felt terrible letting him and his family down as she'd grown very fond of them. Ian had to be back in Malaya in six weeks, and he fully intended to take his new bride with him. As soon as he became a Catholic they were free to marry.

Ian and Molly's wedding took place on 2 February 1952 at St Mary of the Angels Catholic Church in Worthing, Sussex, near to Ian's family home in Ferring-by-Sea. Don and Ciss couldn't get there in time as they were in Singapore, so it was family friend Steve, and not her father, who gave Molly away.

Figure 12.1 Steve about to walk Molly Down the Aisle, 1952

The reception was held at Mitchell's Arcade Café, Worthing. In post-war Britain, only the wealthy could afford elaborate celebrations, so there were only thirty guests, most of whom were family. Even though the war had ended seven years before, dried fruit was still rationed, and unless you hoarded it, there would only be enough to make a one tiered wedding cake. The top half of Molly and Ian's cake was just a prop. Elaborately iced, it was in fact made out of cardboard.

Molly and Ian Cutting the Cake, 1952

Ian was granted an extended leave to allow him to take Molly away on honeymoon. They spent the first part of it driving through Europe, and on 2 May 1952 they set sail for Singapore on the Dutch passenger ship, *Oranje*.

Shortly after the newlyweds arrived in Malaya, Ian was promoted and became Manager on Banir Estate, a 400 acre rubber estate 3 miles to the north of Tapah in the state of Perak. Tapah was the centre of the rubber growing industry, but in 1952 the area was still under siege as it was there that Communist guerrillas had been trying to provoke an uprising. By the time that Molly and Ian were married, the Malayan Emergency had been rumbling on for four years.

Planters who ill-treated their workers were most at risk of reprisals from the insurgents. These tended to be the old Malayan hands who perhaps took their workers for granted. Younger planters like Ian Ripley and Malayan Steve were under constant pressure from their estate owners to increase productivity. And the only way to do that was to ensure that workers' grievances were dealt with as and when they arose. Allowing an industrial dispute to escalate was a mistake that could have fatal consequences.

As the Emergency became more bloody, the police took the precaution of offering better protection to the isolated estate houses. Molly was trained to fire a gun in self-defence and an armed guard accompanied Ian on his estate rounds. Had the insurgents really wanted to, they could have killed many more managers and their families, but they had to win the propaganda war first. Estate workers were leafletted and meetings were held in secret, but while there were many Communist sympathisers in rural areas, in the cities there was less support. Crucially, the Malay ruling class had no time for the Malayan Chinese Communist cause.

One of Japan's justifications for the Second World War had been to overthrow the British power base in Asia and give the power to the workers. But despite three-and-a-half years of Japanese occupation, nothing had changed for the estate workers, most of whom were Tamils originally from Ceylon and southern India. They were still low paid, but at least under the British they had been fed, their children had gone to school, and when they got sick, there was a dispensary where they would be cared for. And it was in the local dispensary, tending workers' wounds, where Molly eventually found her forte and put her nursing training to good use.

It was hard at first for Molly to adjust to life on the estate.

She'd spent ten years in a sociable work environment, but now found herself alone in the daytimes, not even allowed to cook meals as the estate manager's bungalow came with staff. If she wanted to meet anyone or go anywhere, she had to travel with the estate driver as the threat of an ambush made it too dangerous to go out on her own. Even though her parents were not far away in Singapore, it still took a day to travel there.

Despite the Emergency, Molly and Ian did their best to create a semblance of a normal life together. The first entry in Molly's brown leather-bound visitors' book at Banir Estate, Tapah, Perak in 1953 is signed by Ciss and EG Lambert – now MBE. Don had received his award in the New Year's Honours List for 1953. The announcement in *The London Gazette*, 30 December 1952, reads: 'Eric George Lambert Esq, Clerical Officer, Far East Station, Admiralty'. Don had been a loyal servant of the Empire and had been given the honour in recognition for the work he'd done in naval intelligence.

As well as welcoming family and friends to their home, Molly and Ian entertained officials in charge of security for the Tapah area. They were visited by police officers, a major and his deputy from The Worcestershire Regiment, as well as the District Officer. What struck me most when I read the entries in the visitors' book was how many planters there were. It seems nothing short of miraculous that they all survived. Each Sunday they would take turns to host a curry tiffin lunch or would venture out to their club. Despite the dangers, Molly and Ian and their fellow planters were determined to put on a brave face and give each other support.

In late February 1954, my brother was born. Molly was now twenty-seven and the family were still living on Banir Estate. Although she wasn't supposed to walk on her own, she found it very difficult to get the baby off to sleep, and would take him out in his big unwieldy pram and walk through the estate in an effort to get him to nod off.

One evening the little family went out for a walk and wheeled the pram over a makeshift bridge, where armed rebels had been hiding. The rebels, hiding close by, must have known that Ian was the estate manager, but they chose to spare the family's lives. Banir Estate had a far greater prize than the manager and his family, because as well as rubber it had its own tin mine. There was little point going after civilians when you could shoot up an entire British owned mine.

On another occasion, Ian noticed some hastily stubbed out cigarettes lying by the side of the road and contacted the police. The Chinese Communist foot soldiers left clues for the police as they weren't very good at burying their discarded cigarette butts. They smoked a different type of tobacco to the locals too – one that had a distinct acrid scent.

The one job my father dreaded the most during the Emergency was collecting the weekly wages. Every Thursday he would drive to the bank in the armour-plated Land Rover, accompanied by his driver and an armed guard. They would draw out all the money in cash and make their way back to the estate, taking a different route every time, but the armoured vehicle couldn't travel over the rutted tracks faster than 20 miles per hour and it could be seen for miles. Although it was designed to withstand gunfire, it would have been so easy for a heavily armed gang to ambush them, and inside the armoured vehicle they would have been trapped. Even though stealing wages from the mainly Indian estate labourers would have turned public opinion against the rebels, it was only once the workers had been handed their pay packets that Ian could relax – until the following week when he had to do it all over again.

To support the British ground troops, the SAS was

brought in, as well as the RAF and Royal Australian Air Force. Joint aerial bombing raids in one intensive attack destroyed over 180 guerrilla jungle camps, and in 1956 more Commonwealth ground troops were deployed. In total over 500 soldiers, 1,300 police officers and 2,500 civilians were killed. The Malayan Chinese Communists suffered far greater casualties with over 6,000 killed and 1,200 captured.

The Malayan Emergency had much in common with the Vietnam War in that Agent Orange (DDT) was used to clear land and flush out rebels. Also atrocities were committed against innocent people as the Commonwealth troops had trouble distinguishing between Communists and unarmed civilians. The MCP ultimately failed to seize power as it had no support from the Malay community. And even though its members may have been born in Malaya, as ethnic Chinese, they were still seen as outsiders, trying to impose their political will on the Malay people. In the meantime, the Malay elite were content to let British workers, like Ian, carry on helping them rebuild the country after the war, until the time came when they no longer needed them.

CHAPTER 13
– BOARDING SCHOOL

In October 1955, while the Malayan Emergency was still rumbling away, my sister Susan was born. Two years later, Malaya got its independence. As it was no longer a British colony, support for the Malayan ethnic Chinese Communists melted away.

Ian had been promoted and was now manager of Escot Estate on the border of Perak and Selangor, just outside the little town of Tanjung Malim. The family lived in Escot Bungalow, which was not a bungalow at all but a rambling black and white two-storey 1930s house. Molly had been at school in Cameron Highlands with two of the Kennaway girls, who were the first family to live at Escot. I still have the autograph book Molly was given for Christmas 1940 with Susan and Philippa's signatures. The story of the family's dramatic evacuation from Malaya was featured in the book and BBC radio adaptation *Tales from the South China Seas*, and in *Journey by Candlelight*, a memoir written by the eldest daughter, Anne. Their father Mark had volunteered for the army and was captured in 1942 when Singapore fell to the Japanese. Even though Mark had been a prisoer of war in Changi for three years, at the end of the war the Kennaways returned to Escot.

In 1950, the estate was sold. By the time my family arrived to live at Escot, it had been bought by James Warren

& Co, a British rubber firm. Built on flat swampy ground that by then was riddled with mosquitos, the old colonial house was becoming expensive to maintain, and in the heat it was stifling. It was the first home I lived in, although I don't remember it.

As it was cheaper to build a new bungalow than restore the old wooden one, a site was chosen on top of a hill with breathtaking views of the jungle-clad Titiwangsa Mountains. The house was perfect for small children as it was all on one level. A breeze blew through the new Escot Bungalow in the daytime, and at night we had the benefit of modern air conditioners in the bedrooms.

The garden, where my mother grew canna lilies and orchids, sloped down towards a small but deep rectangular swimming pool. It was visible from the house, but there was no fence to stop us wandering down there on our own. I was still in the care of our *amah*, and by then, I suppose, my siblings had learnt to tell a grown-up if we were going swimming. I wasn't afraid of the water, but of the snakes that might have fallen in. I can still picture Velasammy, our cook, running down the garden, broom in hand, alerted by my high-pitched yells.

It was a great honour to be allowed into Velasammy's kitchen. Our parents, whom he called Daddy and Mummy, were kept away; when my mother wanted to learn to cook, Velasammy made up an excuse and shooed her out. Children, though, were allowed into the inner sanctum. I remember sitting on a stool, chewing on a piece of sugar cane while Velasammy amused us with stories, one of which was that the lump in his wrist was a bullet wound from the war. As he deftly kneaded the dough for our bread, the bullet seemed to take on a life of its own and moved around. I could sit and watch it for hours. Whether or not the story was true, it captured our imagination and was a sure fire way of keeping us entertained.

With the Emergency over, we were able, at last, to live a peaceful life, providing we kept away from the wildlife. On Sundays, my father would take us on long walks. We were hoping to see monkeys and apes, in particular gibbons, but one day we got more than we bargained for. My father saw what he thought was a lone male tiger, but when he saw two cubs, he realised to his horror that it was a tigress. He made us hide and prayed the tigress wouldn't catch our scent.

Dad then stepped on to what he thought was a log, but it was, in fact, a hornets' nest. Set upon by an angry swarm, he had to endure the agony of sting after sting without so much as making a sound until the tigers had passed. We managed to stumble home with him, despite his agonising pain, the stings triggering an allergic reaction which had to be treated in the estate dispensary.

Other encounters with the local fauna were a little more light-hearted. My brother had been fishing on Malayan Steve's estate, Sungei Chinoh. Hearing a noise in the undergrowth behind him, he started chatting away to what he thought was his father. But when he turned around, he was confronted by a giant lizard – a water monitor the size of a small crocodile – lumbering through the undergrowth towards him. Terrified, he fell into the water, but fortunately by then our father had heard him and came rushing over to his rescue.

(Figure 13.1 Mum with Hugh, Susan and Alison can be viewed in the gallery section of the website: http://www.lambertnagle.com)

It was an idyllic early childhood, but the rural isolation of Escot meant that there were no suitable schools in the area. As home schooling didn't exist, our only option was boarding school. As the eldest, my brother left for Uplands School in Penang first, followed by my sister Susan. Travelling to school involved a 40 mile car journey to the airport, then a plane ride, followed by a trip up the hill by funicular railway.

Uplands School had been built in the middle of dense jungle on the top of Penang Hill, which at some 2,400 feet soared above the town below, and the only way up and down was by railway. When my sister fell out of a tree and broke her arm, she had to endure a painful journey in a bumpy wooden railway cart before the ambulance could reach her to take her to the hospital.

With her two elder children at boarding school and only me at home for company, Mum found the separation very hard. She'd had to accept that, because of where we lived, there was no alternative but to send her children away, but it didn't make life any easier to cope with and she was having trouble sleeping.

An especially difficult year was 1962. Don, her beloved father, who was by then living in England, died suddenly of a heart attack. Mum worried about her mother, Ciss, now all alone on the other side of the world. In one year she had lost her father, and it seemed her two children had been taken away from her too. At thirty-seven years old, she went to the doctor and was prescribed sleeping pills – the pills she'd taken as a trainee nurse – and, for the first time in her life, anti-depressants.

Mum thought of everything she could to be near her children, to the extent of applying for a job as school nurse at Uplands. When she was offered the post in 1963, she accepted, but with one condition: her four-year-old had to come too.

I was thrilled that I would be going to the same school as my brother and sister. What's more, I believed I would have my mother there with me, not understanding that her job was to look after all the other children. When we got there, I found to my dismay that, even though I was only four, we weren't going to be allowed to live together. Mum had been given her own little bungalow while I had to sleep in a dormitory in the infants school with the other young children, and I wasn't allowed any special treatment just because my mother happened to be the school nurse.

For the first two weeks I cried myself to sleep at night. The infants school can't have been more than fifty yards from the main school, but to me it felt like 500 miles. During the daytimes, I barely saw my mother.

Uplands School, once abandoned and derelict, has been partially restored as the stunning setting and decaying colonial architecture have caught the eye of many a film location scout. It stood in for French Indo-China, now Vietnam, in the movie *Indochine*, and in the television drama hit, *Indian Summers*, it became 1930s Simla, India. When my sister and I first saw the little bungalow our Mum had stayed in featured on screen, it was a shock. Suddenly we were transported back fifty years, and for one crazy moment, I expected to see our mum, in her nurse's uniform, step out through the front door.

Even at a young age, I accepted that I would have to go to boarding school, just like all the other children I knew in Malaya. Set up to educate the children of planters and tin miners, Uplands was pleasant enough. The teachers were kindly and dedicated, as were the staff who cared for us. Set within the grounds were playing fields, where we were encouraged to participate in sports and other outdoor activities. Being so high up, the climate was ideally suited to children who wanted to run and play. I don't recall seeing any child there who was unhappy, once they got over their initial bout of homesickness. We all seem happy enough in our school photographs, including Mum, who loved her job.

Sadly, Uplands didn't have a senior school.

(Figure 13.2 Sister Ripley and Fellow Nurses, Uplands School, Penang can be viewed in the gallery section of the website: http://www.lambertnagle.com)

Mum's Aunt May was a devout Irish Catholic who worried that we three children were in danger of becoming Godless little heathens. May had remained single all her life and now lived as a housekeeper for a wealthy family. All her living costs were paid for so she was able to save every penny, and she decided that her money could be put to good use on a Catholic education for her niece's children. The problem was that a suitable Catholic education didn't seem to exist anywhere nearby. Even Mum's old school, the Pensionnat Notre Dame in Cameron Highlands, had become a non-boarding primary school.

My brother was sent back to England, to Stonyhurst in Lancashire, an elite public school run by the Jesuit order of the Roman Catholic Church. Although the standard of education may have been outstanding, the priests were ill-suited to the pastoral care of their young charges. My brother had to endure harsh corporal punishment, including being given 'six of the best' using a *ferula*, a whale bone covered in leather. I visited Stonyhurst for the first time in the 1990s, and as I stood at the end of the long driveway and looked at the grey stone gothic building, it seemed to me just like a Victorian workhouse.

Susan's school, run by the nuns of the Sacred Heart in Hove, wasn't much better. The nuns seemed intent on removing all the spontaneity and joy from childhood, imposing a strict regime of silence in the corridors. Both children were very unhappy. Their unhappiness became my mother's torment and she continued to take prescribed sleeping tablets, as well as Valium (diazepam) and possibly Librium (chlordiazepoxide) for depression.

Clearly my brother couldn't stay at a school he hated so much, but my parents were divided about what to do for the best. Mum wanted to put him into a day school near Ciss, whereas my father felt that his son was being offered opportunities that he had never had. Not only did he feel obligated to Mum's Aunt May, but he didn't want to offend her. Eventually they decided that Mum would return to England as soon as she could and visit the school in person.

Corporal punishment is now regarded as a form of child abuse, yet it was meted out to children in nearly all schools until the 1970s. And it didn't matter if parents approved or not; there was no law forbidding it and schools didn't need to ask for parental consent. Despite her intervention, it was clear that the school was never going to soften its inhumane regime, but it was only later, when we knew we were going to be moving abroad, that my brother was able to leave.

By the time I was five, my parents, anxious not to repeat the mistakes they'd made with the other two, decided to send me to the local school in Tanjung Malim. The Indian teacher was kind, but the Chinese maths teacher seemed to enjoy hitting the only Western child in the class on the knuckles with a ruler every time I got the answers wrong. Fear doesn't facilitate learning!

The next thing I knew, I too was going to be sent to school in England. I had been to Britain a couple of times by then, and all I could remember was that it was cold. There was an interim period when Mum lived in England and I went to the local school in Ferring, then when I was seven it was my time to go to boarding school. I joined my sister at her new school, the Holy Family Convent in Littlehampton.

The main school, Aucklands, was a Victorian red brick building on a suburban street, set in grounds that extended as far as the sea. For my sister, this was a vast improvement on her last convent, but for me it was an affront. It was far too cold to run around outside the way I'd done in Malaya. I resented the way my freedom had been curtailed and I hated the rigid rules of school life. From when the bell went to rouse us from our beds in the early morning to when I laid my head on my pillow at night, every waking moment of our day was scheduled.

I slept in an iron bed in a dormitory with seven other girls and one nun, Sister Carmel. We were allowed only three items on our bedside table, one of which had to be a hair brush. Sister Carmel had a privacy curtain around her bed, but that made us want to find out what was so mysterious about nuns, and what they wore underneath their habits. We took it in turns to lie underneath the beds to try to see what was going on, but anyone caught doing this, or talking after lights out, was marched straight upstairs in their pyjamas and slippers to stand next to the grandfather clock in the corridor outside the Reverend Mother's office.

The corridor was dimly lit, and it felt scary to be alone at night with nothing to do but listen to the endless tick-ticking of the clock. I didn't like to look down the long, dark corridor in case I saw a ghost. When Reverend Mother did finally emerge, she would tell me that I needed to repent and ask for God's forgiveness. As my penance, she gave me prayers that had to be repeated until I was sufficiently contrite, but all that did was to make me more determined to rebel. Weekends were particularly hard, as after we had done our homework and punishments for various misdeeds (polishing bannisters, cleaning silver), there was very little to do.

Back in Malaya we'd had a menagerie of birds and pets, and I missed them dreadfully. One consolation was that the school had a pet donkey. I would find any excuse to visit his field and pour out my heart about how much I hated being at boarding school while the creature looked at me gravely, as though he was listening.

On Sunday afternoons, we boarders were taken on formal outings. We had to wear our school uniform, which included hats and gloves, in summer and winter, and the nuns took us to visit cheerful places such as dead nuns' graves. What a contrast our lives were to our mum's schooldays.

Our miserable letters home had a profound impact on Mum and caused her much anxiety and turmoil, which she had to hide from us. Instead, she'd write cheerful letters back, full of plans for what we would do when we next saw each other. If only we had been permitted to be weekly boarders, school life would have been so different. Our grandmother Ciss now lived just 6 miles away in Ferring-by-Sea, yet we were only allowed a certain number of weekends away from the school during term time.

In 2014, on a visit to Ferring my sister and I stopped in Littlehampton, curious to find out what had become of our old school. To our astonishment, we couldn't find a trace of the school or its grounds. Torn down in the late 1980s, it had been redeveloped as a housing estate, and not even the nuns' graveyard, a feature of many a dreary Sunday afternoon, remained. It was an odd feeling to stand there and realise that such a big part of our shared history had vanished. If I'd gone to visit on my own, I might have thought I'd dreamt the whole experience.

What is quite uncanny is how little Ferring has changed from when we were small. Ciss had moved there after Don died in 1962. Don had been transferred back to London from Singapore in the early 1960s to serve out his remaining years before retirement, but if he and Ciss had been given a choice, they would happily have stayed in Singapore. They'd spent the best years of their lives in the Far East; to them it was home, and their daughter Molly lived out there too.

Don became a daily commuter up to Admiralty House from the modest home he and Ciss had scraped together the money to buy in Coulsdon, Surrey. They missed the heat, the outdoor life and the colour and vibrancy of the tropics, and cold, grey, miserable England took its toll. Although he was a heavy smoker and drank spirits, Don had always been very slim and outwardly fit, yet he dropped dead from a heart attack at sixty-four. Mum was far away in Malaya when her father died, and both she and Ciss turned to Steve, Don's best friend, for emotional support.

When Ciss bought 2 Ferring Close, Mum and Dad bought number 15, the house opposite, to use as their UK base. My parents set up a family support network in England so that we would have somewhere to go in school holidays, although Mum could only afford to come to England twice a year for the summer holidays and at Christmas. For half terms and spring break, we three children had to be split up.

We would dearly have loved to have flown back to Malaya to see our father. Dad's first employer had allowed him to return to England every summer to see us, but when James Warren & Co took over they immediately put a stop to this. They grudgingly agreed to pay for us to return to Malaya once every three years, but moaned to Dad that his three children cost them too much money. What a contrast in attitude compared with the family-friendly workplaces of today.

My brother went to our favourite grandmother: Mum's mother, Ciss, whom we called Nan Ferring. Susan and I went reluctantly to Dad's parents, Edgar and Maud Ripley, whom we called Nan and Cooker Hassocks. Maud was sweet but downtrodden. We disliked our grandfather as he showed no affection towards us, but he seemed to have a particular problem with male children. His daughter Gill could do no wrong, yet he'd treated his son, my father, badly, and was very unkind to his grandson. Many years after his death we found out that his father had died when he was a little boy and his stepfather had been cruel to him.

Fortunately for my brother, Ciss Lambert was the complete opposite and adored him. Susan and I dreaded it when we had to go and stay at Nan and Cooker's deathly bungalow in Hassocks. When we were in their house we had to be 'seen but not heard'. We were terrified of even using the bathroom before they got up, and one morning my poor sister was so desperate, she jumped out of the bedroom window and weed in the garden.

It was better when they came and stayed in our house in Ferring, although we still had to abide by their strict rules. We would escape to our favourite grandmother's at any opportunity, and envied our brother who, instead of being told off, got thoroughly spoilt. He was even allowed to have breakfast in bed. I suppose this was fair dues, as his school was tougher than ours.

In 1966, neither of our parents were able to return to England to spend the Christmas holidays with us: Dad because he wasn't given any time off, and Mum because she was travelling abroad, looking for a home and business to buy. If it seemed odd to us, I can't imagine how it must have felt for them. It was decided that both sets of grandparents would host Christmas dinner at Number 15 so that we would at least be in our own family home. The two grandmothers, who got on well, were busy preparing the food and setting the table, and my grandfather was, as usual, ordering them about. He did as little to help as possible, but spent his time generally interfering or fussing over the table setting. The only job he was prepared to do was carve the turkey.

The box of Christmas crackers, which contained the party hats, was opened and the crackers were laid carefully at each place setting. We children had been forced to wait to open our presents, and my brother made a play for one of the crackers to be brusquely reprimanded by our grandfather. The crackers weren't to be touched until after the main course.

This wasn't a great start to Christmas lunch. As we sat down to eat, my brother playfully grabbed at another cracker. His authority threatened, our grandfather went berserk. My brother was ordered from the room and told he was to go to bed with no supper as punishment for disobeying. The atmosphere was electric. There was a silence from the rest of us as we stopped and stared in horror. How could anyone be that mean and cold-hearted to a child separated from his parents on Christmas Day?

None of us felt like eating, and we let the meal that our two grandmothers had put so much effort into preparing go cold. Ciss, who was quietly spoken and generally didn't say much, turned to Edgar and asked, "Weren't you ever a little boy?"

Before he could reply, Maud, who was usually too scared of her husband to say anything out of turn, answered for him.

"Yes, and a nasty little one at that."

This childhood memory of the two grandmothers standing up against my grandfather became the basis for the screenplay I wrote for my MA at film school. *Christmas Cracker* was made into a short film and was screened at Leeds Film Festival and in Barcelona. In the fictional version, the heroine leaves her tyrannical husband in search of freedom and a better life, but in real life, my grandmother stayed loyal to her husband for the rest of her days. I'm glad that for one brief moment, she and Ciss stood shoulder to shoulder and gave Edgar his comeuppance.

That incident aside, we looked forward to the holidays, especially over the summer when Mum could come and take care of us. Living together in the same house, coming and going as we pleased, it felt like we were a real family again. We'd spend the summer outside, running free after being cooped up all term.

We put on plays and invited the elderly neighbours to watch, and then had the cheek to charge them. They dutifully sat in our front garden while we performed, my brother and his friend Adam running around with cardboard boxes on their heads. They cut eye holes in the boxes and wrote

BBC on the outside and pretended they were filming.

Adam's mother, Lois, an expat American, and my mum became good friends. I'd never met anyone quite like Lois. She was glamorous, fun-loving and warm-hearted, and was always inviting us to swim in the pool at their holiday house on the sea-front.

However, what we children didn't know was the pressure Dad was under back in what was now Malaysia. The rubber industry was no longer as profitable and his employer needed to make cuts. In a classic case of 'divide and rule', the directors decided that either Ian Ripley or his best friend Ian Stevenson (Malayan Steve) would be selected for redundancy. They chose Dad, using his children's airfares as one expense they could do without, and when the axe finally fell in 1967, it destroyed not only my father's confidence, but also wrecked his one and only true friendship. It was a blow from which my father never truly recovered.

Fed up with being at the mercy of an employer, my parents decided instead to become self-employed and look for an agricultural or horticultural business they could buy. They couldn't afford to buy land in the UK, and so they widened their search area to other English speaking countries. While Dad was finishing up his job, Mum travelled across the world to view the properties they were interested in.

After many weeks on the road, her search ended when she found the perfect house and business: a 26 acre apple and pear orchard in coastal Mariri in the Nelson Bay area of New Zealand. Fellow planters from Malaya had settled in the area and bought similar businesses, so even though my father had never run his own ship, at least with friends close by he wouldn't be short of help and advice.

(Figure 13.3 Molly and Ian's Farewell, Escot Estate, 1967 can be viewed in the gallery section of the website: http://www.lambertnagle.com)

I was in my second year at Holy Family and the end of term was approaching. As usual, I was counting the days to the Christmas holidays when Mum rang me at school with one devastating piece of news about our beloved Labrador retriever, Juba, who had died. As I cried down the phone, she said that she also had some good news that might make Juba's death a little easier to bear: this was to be our last term at boarding school.

Before I could process this, she carried on to say that we wouldn't be going back to Malaya for any more holidays. Instead we would be moving to New Zealand. As people we told kept saying that New Zealand was like England forty years ago, I got a little carried away and convinced myself that everyone there had horses instead of cars. I built my own 'castle in the air', imagining a land where boarding schools hadn't yet been invented, and decided then and there that I loved this new place.

CHAPTER 14
– A BRIEF ENCOUNTER

Throughout her married life, Mum was in close touch with her friend Steve, but she'd kept this a secret from my father. When Mum received letters in Malaya from her mother, Ciss, Steve's letters would be hidden inside. I expect Dad thought that once Mum was married, she and Steve would stop writing to each other, but Steve was her rock, there whenever she'd needed emotional support. And Steve was a habit she just couldn't seem to break.

Ciss was good at keeping secrets. She'd proved that by keeping quiet about her war work. When we asked her what she did in the war, she would smile at us, put her finger to her lips, and say, "codes and ciphers." And that would be the end of the conversation. Now, however, she was being asked to keep her daughter's secret from her son-in-law, whom she loved.

Mum tried to convince herself that Steve was a benevolent uncle and father-figure. She didn't want to hurt Dad either, but trying to conceal the relationship backfired. When Dad finally did find out, he was convinced that there was more to it than Mum let on.

Mum reached out to Steve when her beloved father died suddenly and her world fell apart. Ciss and Don had been devoted to each other and had been looking forward to their retirement when Don was so cruelly taken. Mum, who was in Malaya at the time, was desperately worried about her mother, and Steve had been Don's best friend. It was Steve who helped organise the funeral, advised Ciss on her finances and took care of all the practical and administrative tasks of sudden death.

On our last visit to London before we left for New Zealand, Mum broke the news to Steve that we were leaving for good. I remember that day vividly. Although she had to put a positive spin on the move for the sake of her children, with Steve Mum could drop the pretence. And in that fleeting moment that I witnessed, where she'd clung to Steve so desperately, it was tearing her apart. Mum didn't want to move to New Zealand, she didn't want to leave Ciss on her own, and I'm convinced she didn't want to let go of Steve.

As much as she loved her husband and family, I realise Mum had a deep and enduring love for Steve too. What was it, this bond they had? I tried to read between the lines in the letters Mum wrote. They seemed at ease in each other's company, shared a similar sense of humour and enjoyed exchanging gossip about mutual friends. But as I look back now, they didn't seem to have much else in common, and had opposing personalities. But then you could say the exact same thing about my father. I suspect that my parents were two people who wanted opposite things in life too.

Steve was fogeyish and formal, while Mum was spontaneous. She was an extrovert who liked socialising, while he enjoyed solitary pursuits such as photography. Mum was sporty and loved dancing, but Steve felt uncomfortable and awkward on the dance floor. And he barely got out for a round of golf.

After his years of working in the Far East in wartime, Steve wanted to take life a little easier. Meanwhile, Mum was busy grabbing life by both hands, eager to pursue a nursing career. Although a fifteen year age gap meant more then than it would today as male life expectancy was so much lower, it wasn't their difference in age that was significant, but their attitude.

I think it was her desire to have a family that ultimately drove Mum to look for someone closer to her in age. And perhaps she feared being left on her own in later life. From Steve's perspective, he may have felt that it would have been an act of disloyalty, as Don's best friend, to have pursued a relationship with Don's daughter.

(Figure 14.1 Norman Stephens, 1920s can be viewed in the gallery section of the website: http://www.lambertnagle.com)

When I first opened Mum's pocket diary for 1968, inside the front cover was a photograph of Steve as a young man, a tiny keepsake she had kept hidden away. I'd been puzzling over the initials NDES, embossed on the brown leather cover. And then I realised that they were Steve's, Norman David Stephens, (although I don't know what the E stood for).

The last note Mum wrote in that diary before we left England was on 12 January, 1968, when she took her car up to London to sell it. When the day came for us to leave, my sister remembers that it was Steve who drove us all to Tilbury docks to catch our ship. Steve had always been very kind to Susan and me, even though we were rather ungrateful. It was our way of showing that we resented the hold he had over our mother. He presented us both with watches as going away presents. I have no recollection of it, but Susan recalls being kissed firmly on the cheek as he bid her goodbye. She found the sensation unpleasant.

But the most difficult goodbye of all was for Mum. Thirty years since she'd left from these very same docks as an eleven-year-old girl, here she was again, setting off on another journey into the unknown. Only this time she had deep misgivings.

We sailed on the SS *Rangitane* and made our way down

towards the Bay of Biscay, where we hit a storm. While Susan and I lay groaning in our bunks, Mum was a good sailor and rough seas didn't bother her. Her mood lifted and she threw herself into all the games and activities on board, popping back every now and again to the cabin, armed with the prizes she'd won at deck games, to see how we were.

Once we left the Bay of Biscay, the sea became calmer and we were able to get up and join in the entertainment on board. We arrived at our first port of call, Curacao in the Dutch Caribbean, on Sunday 28 January. Mum noted the date in her diary as there was another letter from Steve waiting for her, the third letter he'd written to her that month. As the ship sailed into port, we stood on deck admiring the colourful wooden houses, but we stopped in port only for as long as it took to load fresh supplies and new passengers.

At Panama City two days later, there was another letter from Steve. I remember trailing around the streets, which seemed to be full of bearded men in green army uniforms carrying guns, and it was a relief to get back on the ship. We watched from the deck as we sailed through the Panama Canal, the jungle clad shoreline reminding me of the Malaysia I'd left behind.

As the ship left the canal for the open sea, the first sighting of the vast Pacific Ocean, stretching out in endless blue, marked a turning point in our journey. We'd passed the halfway point and now we were at last heading to our new home.

The final port of call, ten days later, was Papeete in Tahiti. To most people, a day at the beach in a tropical paradise would be their idea of heaven, but 11 February 1968 happened to be a Sunday, when all the banks were closed. My mother had got off the ship with sterling, and none of the restaurants or hotels would change it for her. Credit cards didn't exist then and we were stuck at a beach resort for the whole day with no funds.

All Mum wanted to buy was some shade: somewhere for me to sit when the sun was at its fiercest. I had inherited my father's fair skin, while Mum had taken after her father and tanned easily. Beaches back in Malaysia had palm trees for me to shelter under, but this one had no shade whatsoever, and the only respite from the relentless sun was under the terrace of the resort hotel nearby. In this French colonial outpost the waiters refused my mother's English money, and wouldn't allow us to sit in the shade for free. The hotel catered for well-off French tourists and families weren't the sort of guests they wanted there.

I spent the day swimming and running in and out of the water. I had covered up with a tee-shirt, but the sun's rays burnt straight through it, and that night, back on board ship, my back swelled up into an enormous blister. The ship's doctor gave me injections of what must have been morphine. He'd never seen such a bad case of sunburn, and I remember to this day the warning he gave me about never allowing myself to get burnt like that again. I couldn't lie on my back for the rest of the trip and Mum had to give me sponge baths as showering was too painful. She was beside herself with worry and guilt, blaming herself for having the wrong currency, but it had hardly been her fault.

When the ship finally arrived in Wellington a week later, I had recovered sufficiently to get excited. My father and brother had flown directly from Malaysia and met us when the ship docked. As Susan and I hadn't seen Dad in months, we couldn't wait to tell him about our trip, and I blurted out news of our visit to London to see Uncle Steve.

I didn't have to say any more. Even mentioning Steve's name made my father unhappy and his forehead was a knot of anger and hurt, yet I hadn't set out deliberately to upset him. He said nothing apart from, "Did you? That's interesting," as we hadn't seen each other for so long and he didn't want to spoil our reunion. Dad had gone to the trouble of finding an Indonesian restaurant close to the hotel that served the same food as we'd eaten in Malaysia for our first meal together. But, like the rest of our family, he wasn't very good at hiding his feelings.

The next day we set off on our final sea voyage, this time on the three hour ferry crossing across Cook Strait to South Island. From Picton, it was a two-and-a-half hour drive on a twisty road. The car came to a halt at last at Ruby Bay, outside a nondescript pink concrete bungalow on the shoreline. Not quite the ornate ruby-encrusted Hansel and Gretel house I'd imagined, lying on my front in my bunk on the ship, unable to sleep because of the pain from the sunburn.

As soon as I woke up the next morning, I was impatient to go gem collecting. Instead of the pale white sand of my imagination, the beach was grey and stony. No matter how hard I looked, none of those grey and black pebbles ever did reveal a ruby nestling in their midst. This was a major setback, as in my head I'd already collected my rubies, traded them in for a pile of banknotes then promptly gone out and bought a pony.

Mum had learned to ride at her convent in Malaya and shared her passion for horses with me. I'd spent as much free time as money would allow at the riding school in Ferring, and one of the major attractions of our new house and orchard was the 9 acres of grazing land that came with it. But for the first three months, while we were in the rented house, I had to be content with the imaginary horses in my favourite children's poem: 'White Horses' by Irene Pawsey. As I looked at the waves, I saw their white manes waving in the wind and imagined them galloping under the sea to their stable in the watery underworld.

For my parents, facing up to their new lives as orchardists, reality came as a shock. During their first fruit season, they learnt the ropes from the outgoing owners, but I don't think any of us, apart from my father, understood what a grind it was to harvest fruit. As owner-managers, Dad and Mum would be hands-on, and I'm sure Mum hadn't factored in how hard the work would be. On Easter Monday, 15 April 1968, she wrote that she had worked all day picking apples, but had fallen off her ladder in the morning and received some nasty bruises.

Climbing up and down ladders carrying a laden bag of apples for eight hours a day was exhausting. And as we constantly had to move the ladder around on uneven ground, it was inevitable that sometimes we fell off. Ladders had a habit of toppling over on top of us when we had a full bag of fruit, and never, it seemed to me, when the bag was empty. It wasn't the damage we did to ourselves we worried about, but the loss of all that export quality fruit, which would then have to be sent to the canning factory.

Even though the work was repetitive and tiring, with the right company it could be fun. I can't say that Mum ever liked the manual work on the orchard, but she did enjoy the camaraderie when the international backpackers came to work for us. Many of them were professionals taking a career break, and Mum loved to talk to them about the countries they came from and their way of life back home.

That first year on the orchard, Mum was constantly tired, and she found it difficult to keep up with all the chores she had to do. Once the fruit season was over at the end of May, we were at last able to move into our new house over three days in early June. Mum and Dad combined their first names and called their business Marian Orchards. Our house was a rambling black and white two-storey weatherboard, built in the 1930s on a gentle slope, facing towards Kina Peninsula. We were 6 miles from the town of Motueka and 1 mile from the nearest shop, post office and primary school at Tasman.

Once we'd moved to Marian Orchards, for my ninth

birthday I was finally allowed a pony. There were, though, conditions attached. I would have to see to his needs before and after school, even if it meant getting up early. It was a big responsibility for a nine-year-old, but I was determined to prove to my parents that I was capable.

Apart from noting dental appointments and a parents' evening, Mum barely had time to write in her 1968 diary. She was so preoccupied with the daily grind, she failed to note that New Zealand was hit by two major disasters not long after we arrived. In April 1968, the inter-island ferry *Wahine* sank in Wellington Harbour in a ferocious storm. Fifty-one people drowned. A month later, less than 100 miles from where we lived, three people were killed and seventy per cent of the town of Inangahua was destroyed in an earthquake measuring 7.1 on the Richter scale.

I remember being woken up (it was 5.24am) by a deep rumbling noise, followed by the room shaking. In the kitchen there was a storage cabinet made out of glass where we kept crockery and crystal, and the rattle and crack from that was alarming as the glasses began to shatter. The shaking seemed to go on forever, although in reality it lasted for scarcely two minutes.

The rhythm of our lives was governed by the seasons. And even in the winter there were jobs to do on the orchard. Once the fruit had been picked, the trees had to be pruned. In the winter the staff accommodation had to be maintained, all the machinery on the orchard had to be serviced, and there were directives from the fruit industry governing body to implement. Then there was a month's respite, after pruning in midwinter at the end of July, when orchardists were able to take some time off.

On top of the hard physical graft, there was the business side to run. It was in the evenings and on Saturday afternoons after work that Dad had to do all the administration – including bookkeeping, invoices and the wages. In

October and November, my mother would help him recruit the staff for the picking season.

As we were producing prime fruit for the export market, my father had to follow a strict regime of chemical spraying, which he started once the fruit began to develop. One insecticide which we all hated was Gusathion. My father had to drive the sprayer up and down every row of trees until he'd covered all 26 acres. He wore a mask, but the spray got in his hair and must have been absorbed through his skin. Before spraying we had to move all our animals as far away from the orchard as possible, and do everything we could to prevent spray drift tainting not only the pasture, but our own water supply.

Perhaps it is little wonder that the agonising sinus headaches Dad had suffered all his life became more frequent. It had been hard work keeping profits up during his twenty years as a planter, but on the rubber estate he'd had other people to do the manual labour for him. That left him free to concentrate on overseeing the operation and the strategic management of the business. As an orchardist in New Zealand, he was expected to do everything. During the season, which ran from December to the end of May, Dad worked a six-day-week, just as he'd done in Malaya for all those years.

As anyone who has ever run a horticultural business will know, the one thing that you wish you could control, more than anything, is the weather. From September through to May, there was constant worry that a storm or unseasonal hail would wipe out the entire crop. Perhaps as a way of taking his mind off the stress of running the orchard, in what little spare time he had, my father was always making something for us children. He built us a table tennis set, had our tennis court resurfaced as it had been damaged during the earthquake, and even bought us a boat and waterskis.

Every year in spring, something magical happened that

made even my overworked father a little more cheerful. The air would be full of the scent of fragrant apple blossom and the entire orchard would be festooned in the palest white and pink flowers. With spring came the hope for an abundant pip fruit season, as once the blossom fell off the trees, the apples started to appear. In late spring, the next job on the orchard was 'thinning', leaving only the best fruit so that they could grow to the right size.

December 1968 marked the start of our second season on the orchard, and once the school holidays began we were all expected to pitch in and help. Mum worked in the packing shed grading apples, and as I wasn't strong enough to carry a bag of apples, I worked there too. I was too small to reach the apples out of the bin so had to stand on a box, wrapping the fruit in purple tissue paper then placing it in rows in a protective layer of cardboard. Five or six layers later, the whole box was packed and ready for export. It was repetitive but satisfying work as I knew I was earning money to pay for my pony's upkeep. I acquired a work ethic at age nine, and I am immensely grateful to my parents for that.

While we three children loved our new life, Mum was struggling. She was forty-two, working full time on the orchard, running a five bedroom house and cooking for a family. It was the first time she'd ever had to look after a house of that size without help, and we didn't employ so much as a cleaner. My father not only did his share of the household chores, he was the one who taught Mum to cook. We children had our own jobs, from collecting eggs from our chickens to cleaning out the fireplace and bringing in the wood in the winter.

Mum was careful to keep her problems to herself as she was afraid she'd be condemned as a spoilt colonial who couldn't even manage a house without servants. Women in rural New Zealand were capable and resourceful, but the social rules appeared to hark back to the 1950s, where gender roles were strictly defined. All the women Mum met seemed to spend their days bottling fruit or making jam, whereas she had grown up in urban Hong Kong and Singapore and had been brought up to pursue a career. And she wasn't about to turn into a domestic goddess in her forties.

(Figure 14.2 Molly with Shaun can be viewed in the gallery section of the website: http://www.lambertnagle.com)

Once when Mum was invited out to a coffee morning, the invitation had read 'Ladies, a Plate', and that was exactly what she brought with her – a Royal Doulton china plate. It was only when she got there that she realised all the other women had brought a perfectly filled homemade sponge cake or a plate of freshly baked biscuits. But Mum was ever resourceful and found ways of passing off cakes and biscuits she'd bought from a bakery as her own. Or she would make marmalade and pretend that she'd been slaving over the stove for hours, when in truth she'd added water to the contents of a kit and gone out to walk the dog. These were small but feisty victories, and her defiant stand makes me laugh when I look back now.

Luckily for Mum, the Nelson area in the early 1970s was changing, attracting an eclectic mix of expats from Europe: bohemian artists and potters, drawn there by the beautiful scenery and lovely climate. Mum made friends easily and loved socialising. In rural New Zealand, we had to make our own entertainment. We would host or be invited to curry tiffin with ex-planter friends and talk about the good old days in Malaya.

There were mixed fortunes amongst these families. One couple had bought an orchard with old stock and then had to replace the trees. They'd struggled to make enough money to keep the business going and were forced to sell at a loss. Another friend suffered a life-changing tractor accident when out on the orchard.

By the early 1970s, we had owned the orchard for nearly five years and my parents were exhausted. The work was relentless, and it was clear by then that it was never going to get any easier. This put Mum and Dad's relationship under severe strain, and for the sake of their marriage they needed to find a way of keeping the house and selling off the business as a going concern. It was make or break time for both of them.

PART 3
1968–2015

CHAPTER 15
– IN GOD'S COUNTRY

Mum had become increasingly frustrated that her professional skills were going to waste, and in the early 1970s she talked about returning to nursing. I think she was trying to prove to us, and to herself, that she hadn't left it too late. And she still had a desire within her to feel needed now that her eldest child had flown the nest. Even if she wasn't conscious of it at the time, I think that nursing was a way to reconnect with her younger, happier self.

There was a job vacancy for a midwife at Motueka Maternity Hospital and we encouraged her to apply. I hoped that by going back to nursing, Mum would feel more settled. And we'd all benefit as that would improve the atmosphere at home. When she was down, she would snap at us for no apparent reason, and the slightest comment could set her off. She'd yell at Dad that she hated New Zealand, she wanted to go back to live in England and it was all his fault that she was so unhappy, but when she was up, she was the life and soul of any social gathering. Her friends referred to her as 'Jolly Molly'.

Before Mum was allowed to practise as a midwife, she had to complete further professional development. That entailed six months more training, and the nearest course was at a hospital 150 miles away, across the sea in Wellington, but if it meant Dad, Susan and I had to fend for ourselves, I was happy to do so. I was thirteen and had been taught to cook at primary school, and I was keen to try out my skills.

I'd recently returned home from a disastrous stint at boarding school, where I had lasted just three weeks. I had survived two boarding schools by the age of thirteen, but I wasn't tough enough for this one. The staff had rigged up an intercom surveillance system in the dormitories, which was turned on after lights out. Every whisper, cuss or remark would be picked up. If we said anything derogatory about the school, the prefect on duty would recognise our voices, haul us out of bed and report us to the Matron, who would dish out various punishments.

I felt like I was in prison, not school, being spied on in this way, and my unhappiness began to affect my school work, but I couldn't tell Mum and Dad what was going on as we weren't allowed home until half-term. There was no point trying to send a private letter from the school as letters were censored by a prefect first. And we couldn't make a private phone call from the hostel as someone was always listening. It seemed that the staff did everything in their power to thwart me, but I had to get out of there.

I spotted my chance one Sunday morning on my way to church. As one of the few Catholics at this Anglican school, I was allowed off the premises to go to mass, but I had to wear school uniform, presumably so that I could be identified if I ran away. My salvation was a public telephone box. I'd brought coins for the church collection box, but I'm afraid that when the time came to give money, I pretended I didn't have any. Then, as soon as the priest told the congregation that we could leave, I was off.

I only had this one chance, but when I got to the pay phone, there was a man in there having a leisurely conversation, smiling as though he didn't have a care in the world. All I could think about was what would happen to me if I was late back. The minutes ticked by, then at last he hung up.

My hands were shaking so much that I could barely dial the number. I prayed it would be Dad who answered, but I got Mum, and I'd caught her in a bad mood. She told me I'd have to stick with it, that it would get better and not to squander my chances at the best school in the district. She just didn't seem to get it.

And then Dad came on the phone. I pleaded with him to come and take me away, and when he heard how we were being treated, he dropped everything. He told me to go back to the school and wait for him.

I arrived back to a reception committee and was told to report to the Matron. I'd been spotted outside the phone box by a nosy Old Girl, who'd recognised the uniform and had promptly reported me to the school. And I had some explaining to do. But before Matron could dish out yet more petty punishments, my father swept up the drive in his grey Jaguar and told her exactly what he thought of her bugging device.

I by then had run upstairs. Never have I packed a suitcase at the speed I did that day, flinging items of clothing in one after the other, sitting on my case to fit everything in then dragging it downstairs before Dad could change his mind. As we drove off, all the boarders were hanging out the windows, thrilled, no doubt, at all the excitement.

So having gone through all that, Mum going off on a course for six months was really no big deal for me. My sister was still at home in her final year at school, and we had Dad to look after us. We went to visit Mum in Wellington to meet all the new friends she'd made on the course, and when she came home to see us she seemed buoyed up by her experience.

In 1973 Mum, Dad and I made our first visit back to the UK in five years. A few days before we were due to leave,

I put what I thought was a temporary rinse in my hair to brighten it up, but as the colour dried it began to take on the hue of an amber traffic light. I realised at that point that there had been a mix up with the labels and the colour was permanent.

I made a desperate attempt to cover my head with scarves and hats, but no matter what I did, I couldn't disguise the dreadful mess I'd made. I felt sick; I knew Dad would be furious with me, and I braced myself for the inevitable. Sure enough, he hit the roof, telling me I looked like a trollop and that he was too ashamed to take me to England to meet our relatives. Mum did her best to be the peacemaker; she knew I hadn't done it deliberately and that I wasn't trying to sabotage the trip. I skulked around the house, but I still had to face him at supper.

We were flying via the United States, as Dad had always wanted to visit: he liked the work ethic and 'can-do' attitude. By the time we flew to San Francisco we had made our peace. We ate sourdough bread and seafood at Fisherman's Wharf, drove over the Golden Gate Bridge and rode in a cable car. And then came the excitement of New York, where we walked round Times Square and took a ferry to the Statue of Liberty. We'd left our cares behind and for those few days not a cross word was spoken, but as soon as we checked in for our flight to the UK, my father received a telegram asking him to take the next plane.

Dad's mother had been in and out of hospital and had been steadily going downhill. She had taken a turn for the worse, and we were now on a mercy dash. There were no spare seats in economy, so British Caledonian flew us First Class and the captain sent a message to the hospital, telling them we were on our way. Dad's mother, whom he and Mum called Marsie, clung to life when she heard that, and once we landed, we drove straight to her bedside.

Even though she could barely lift her head off the

pillow, she turned her head as Dad entered the ward and her eyelids fluttered at the sight of her beloved son. He had done as he'd promised and was able to fulfil his dying mother's one last wish.

Being in England unsettled us, and Mum in particular found it hard when we got back to New Zealand. She had got the job at the maternity hospital in Motueka, but as she was new, she was given the graveyard shift that nobody else wanted. And as no one was in any hurry to retire, Mum worked four nights, week in, week out. All she wanted was equal treatment with her colleagues; all management did was fob her off.

Night duty wreaked havoc on her body clock. She was tired and often irritable. She'd always had trouble sleeping, but had coped with the occasional restless night. However, trying to sleep in the daytime, knowing she had to get up for work that evening, was different. As a regular long-haul flyer I know how jet lag can mess with my body clock in a similar way. It takes me five nights to resume a regular sleeping pattern after flying to the other side of the world, and if I had to do that every week I know just how desperate I would feel.

Clinical research by neuroscientists is challenging the assumption that the human body can adapt to working a night shift. As researchers begin to understand the mechanism of sleep and what happens when sleep goes wrong, they are concluding that daytime sleep is not nearly as beneficial to health as sleeping at night. Professor Russell Foster, speaking on *The Night Shift* on BBC Radio 4, said that night shift workers had impaired cognitive function as severe as someone who was drunk. Professor Michael Hastings, an expert in the twenty-four-hour body clock, went on to state that because of our evolutionary biology, the body is hardwired to perform certain functions at particular times of the day and night.

Mum tried everything to get to sleep, from lining the bedroom curtains with blackout fabric to installing air-conditioning to drown out noise. She would lie there, trying to rest, but was kept awake by her thoughts. And because she had to sleep for work, she turned to pills.

I was twelve when I first became aware that the medicine cabinet in the bathroom was groaning under the weight of pill bottles and medicines. I thought that my mum stored all these tablets because she was a nurse, although the only other medical family I knew kept their drugs locked away in their surgery.

She was prescribed a type of anti-anxiety medication, benzodiazepines. A sedative with hypnotic effects, it could be used to treat insomnia, but was meant for short-term use only. The brand she took was Mogadon, and it made her feel so groggy and bad-tempered when she woke up that she started taking uppers to get her through the day.

She got some of her pills from her own GP, but given the different combinations of drugs she took, she must have been getting her fix from a doctor or chemist in another town. A patient's notes were kept in a paper filing system by each surgery, and there was no centralised database that would alert a doctor if their patient was consulting more than one GP at a time. The system relied on trust.

Mum wrote down every tablet she took in forensic detail, just as she would have done for one of her patients. She self-medicated to do her job and derived no pleasure from the tablets. And from the research I've carried out in the course of writing this book on drug use in the medical profession, she was far from being the only one. One article called self-medication by healthcare workers a 'silent epidemic' and said that it was a major health risk for nurses. All drugs have side-effects; Mum knew that from nursing training. And pharmacology, the study of drugs, derives from the Greek word, *pharmakon*, meaning poison.

Mum began recording her dreams, which were basically psychedelic drug trips, in 1975. She was by this time forty-nine and was struggling with the symptoms of the menopause, having hot flushes and fretting about losing her looks. She still loved to dress up for special occasions, but the opportunities were rare in rural New Zealand, and she remembered a dream where she was with friends from Malaya. They showed her a lovely photograph of her young self in evening dress, looking glamorous.

She was still taking nitrazepam, but one tablet no longer worked, so she upped her dose to two and took them with two other sleeping tablets, sold as Tricloryl. After mixing her medication she had a distressing dream about our two cats. They were in prison behind a barbed wire fence, being kept against their will. Another time Mum dreamt about her sister-in-law, Gill. The family was gathered around the bedside of Pop Ripley, Dad's father, who had died earlier in the year. Mum wrote that in the dream, *Ian and Gill had a big reunion and a sort of truce.* It was classic wish-fulfilment as Dad and my aunt had had a big falling out. Mum was on good terms with her sister-in-law and loved her two little nieces dearly, and she thought that life was too short for family feuds.

That was a good life lesson I learned from her.

Mum was often late in real life and had an anxiety dream that involved missing a train and losing me and Susan in London.

I wandered all over the nightclubs and go-go dancing places to find them, and it was awful going from place to place.

We would have dropped everything to be with Mum if she'd asked. Only she never did. Even though she missed us terribly when we moved to England, she was the one who'd brought us up to stand on our own two feet. And if that meant living far away from her, that was the price she paid for bringing her children up to be independent.

One night she dreamt about Fred, the vicar's son whom she'd been engaged to when she met Dad. In her dream, she promised to go back and marry him. And Dad had given her permission to go. She wrote that she was about forty-two in the dream and all three of us children were grown up.

I had this awful pink wedding dress. We all went to the beach somewhere. Then we went back to Fred's house and his mother was there. She was so nice – rather like the mother in 'Family at War'. Anyway, I told Mrs Sherman why I let Fred down. I said I was all mixed up about leaving Ian and my three children, and anyway I was a bit old to start again. Then I caught sight of Fred looking down at me from a window. He watched me wash the kitchen floor and suddenly I felt young and attractive.

When Mum woke up, she was relieved that it had been a dream. Dad was there beside her and all the confusions and decisions had been fictional. As she admitted, she'd taken too many sleeping tablets that night.

On 4 December, Mum wrote, *had the most awful row we've ever had*. She compared it to her other arguments with Dad. The worst that had happened up to then was that she'd thrown a cup of coffee and Dad's pipe at him, and dropped his plate of egg and bacon deliberately on the floor.

Thank God Alison wasn't there. I screamed and went for him with a spanner. He twisted my arms and told me to pack my bags and leave. I'm bruised all over today. Please God we don't have another one. He said he didn't mean what he said, but I know the score is against me.

This wasn't the father I knew and loved. I don't believe he meant to hurt her, but a line had been crossed. Both Mum and Dad had proved that, given the right provocation, they were capable of using physical violence against each other.

Mum was both frightened and ashamed at the depths they had sunk to and blamed herself. She listed two reasons for the row, the first of which was Steve. Steve had died that year, yet my father was still jealous of him. He had been found dead of a heart attack or stroke in his flat in Kensington, and no one had noticed that he was missing for three days. It was his lonely death, more than anything, that had cut Mum to the quick, but my father wasn't able to cope with the deep feelings Mum still held for Steve. He'd known about Steve when they first met, but Mum had played down the relationship, insisting that Steve was a father figure. Perhaps she thought that marriage to Dad would allow her to let Steve go finally, but no matter how hard she tried, there was still an emotional connection. Even after he died, she couldn't stop thinking about him.

The second reason, an incident on the SS *Rangitane*, is more intriguing. This was the first time that Susan or I knew that Mum had met someone on board our ship. Although the three of us shared the same cabin, we kept different hours and there were plenty of opportunities for her to slip away in the evenings after we'd gone to bed. As a Catholic, Mum believed that no matter what sins you had committed, provided you confessed and were contrite, you would be redeemed and forgiven. Despite his conversion to the Catholic faith, deep down Dad wasn't so forgiving. He couldn't let go of past hurts and had lost the ability to live in the moment.

I can see these now as symptoms of his depression. I can't remember exactly when I became aware that Dad was becoming increasingly withdrawn, but I thought that if I was cheerful around him it might make him feel better. When that didn't work, I began to worry.

CHAPTER 16
– SPIRAL

The year 1976 started with a Hogmanay party where Mum and Dad had such a good time Scottish country dancing they didn't get home until 2am. Then they stayed up until 4.30am talking about the past.

Mum was still recording her dreams, and in February she had an anxiety dream about work. She had fused all the lights and had to fumble around in the dark with the premature babies she was looking after. She tried to carry two babies at a time out of the nursery, but the floor was slippery and she fell by the incubator.

I didn't drop the babies.

Three months later, she had another stress-related dream about the very pills that were meant to be helping her. In the dream she tried to conceal her drug habit – packing up and hiding all her tablets before anyone found out. She'd taken a trycylic anti-depressant, Surmontil, but despite its other adverse side-effects (memory loss, dizziness and blurred vision), it wasn't supposed to give the patient unpleasant dreams. Yet Mum had disturbed sleep, where in her mind she had a fight with Dad and threw a couple of pots and pans at him. This was followed by another anxiety dream about nearly missing a plane.

The drugs, it seemed, no longer worked:

Can't seem to get a decent sleep lately.

In mid-June Mum wrote she had a mad dream that Dad and Fred met. She was surprised as they seemed to get on. Then a few days later she was dreaming about Steve. She refers to him as 'Uncle', yet it had been thirty years or more since she'd last called him that.

Had a horrible dream about Uncle Steve rejecting me. I was looking absolutely gorgeous and he met me at the station. He said I could spend the night at his house, but he was very cold and indifferent, and obviously had no time for me anymore. I have come down from my pedestal now alright.

Now that Steve was dead, Mum no longer had any man in her life prepared to overlook her faults and love her unconditionally. Dad had done so once, but after twenty-five years of marriage, their relationship was straining under the weight of all that life had thrown at them.

On 22 June, Mum took one-and-a-half Mogadon with the sleeping tablet Trichloryl which gave her another anxiety dream about being late. She dreamt that Dad had sent her to meet her sister-in-law, Gillian, off a plane in Malaysia.

I turned away and met a very attractive and pleasant man (in his fifties) who suggested we go somewhere and have a drink. We did, and then went for a walk along the beach. By the time I got back it was to find the plane had taken off with Gillian and without me. I spent the rest of the dream trying to catch her up at various places, but never succeeding, and I was afraid to go back to Ian. I knew he would give me the most terrible telling off for leaving her, not to mention going and having a drink with this man. Woke up feeling awful (too many tablets). I must cut down on them. They are ruining my life.

Mum's good intentions to cut down on the pills never came to anything. The grind of four nights on duty, week after week, defeated her. But much as she hated the personal toll night duty took on her health, she loved the job. We couldn't walk down the high street without a proud parent stopping us to show off a growing infant Mum had delivered.

One type of drug she took gave her hallucinogenic dreams, like this one:

...huge jet aeroplanes shaped like air balloons just above my head.

She dreamt that she was taking my brother as a little boy to Euston station, where he had to catch his train to boarding school. Then she has another wish-fulfilment dream about Steve.

I decided to call in and see Steve and he asked me to marry him, but said I must finish school first. We went somewhere in a train in a double bed.

Other less disturbing dreams reflected her day-to-day life – anxiety dreams about work and one about a colleague who she knew didn't like her.

From 1977 onwards, Mum put aside her dream diary and started writing frankly about her life, her children and the difficulties she was having with Dad. She was pleased to have my sister home for the holidays, and on Monday 3 January they went swimming and sunbathing at Kina, our nearest beach.

Swimming in the sea made Mum happy in a way that none of the mood-altering drugs ever could. She was on duty for four consecutive nights that week and needed the swim to get her through her shifts, but the beneficial effect of the dip was short-lived. The next morning she woke up in a bad mood. She'd only worked one night and there were still three more to go.

She made egg and bacon pie for supper that evening, but berated herself for her poor pastry making skills. When she wrote in her diary the next day, describing her night at work, Mum said that her boss, Sister H, had been very friendly, noting down that it didn't happen often.

After going to sleep for a few hours, Mum woke up

feeling groggy, but instead of taking it easy, she drove to Nelson with my sister. Tired from the trip, she realised she needed more sleep to function. She took two red bombs (the barbiturate Soneryl) and slept for five hours, before getting up for night duty. When I read Mum's diaries, I realised that she had taken benzodiazepines and how harmful they were. But when I found out about the barbiturates as well, I understood for the first time why I could never wake her up.

In Mum's belated list of New Year's resolutions, there is no mention of cutting down her drugs. She intended to make jam and preserves, as well as take up a new hobby: dressmaking or further education by correspondence. Two of her resolutions concerned Dad. She wanted to persuade him to have visitors around more often, and help him lose weight. Dad did have an underactive thyroid which made him lethargic, but he also had a habit of eating when he was anxious – as I did too.

I left for a trip to Australia in mid-January, and was planning to meet up with Mum in Queensland, where my brother was getting married. Mum felt restless when I left and found it hard to sleep. Unfortunately that meant she took an ever more potent drug cocktail of two barbiturates and one-and-a-half benzodiazepines, washed down with one-and-a-half tablets of amphetamine and barbiturate. She called them 'blues', but they're better known as 'purple hearts'. Amphetamine, the stimulant, was supposed to elevate mood, while the barbiturate was meant to counter the side effects of the stimulant.

My sister recalls a conversation she had with Mum. Mum told Susan that she'd first been prescribed purple hearts in Malaya, which suggests to me that she took them for depression when my brother and sister were sent away to school.

Mum had been home from Australia for less than a

day when, in the early hours of 1 February 1977, one day before their Silver Wedding anniversary, Dad tried to take his own life. He'd swallowed forty sleeping tablets: twenty Mogadon and twenty Trichloryl, and the only reason he didn't die right there and then was thanks to the merciful intervention of his GP. A kind, caring and compassionate man, the GP was the one person my deeply troubled, depressed father could confide in.

Dad had for so many years been bottling up his troubles, and this was a cry for help. When he talked to Mum about why he had done it, he told her it was so that she could be free. We were very, very lucky not to have lost him that day.

Because of the stigma surrounding mental health at that time, Mum shouldered this terrible burden, concealing it from her two elder children. They were both working away, making their way in the world in demanding professions, and Mum didn't know what else to do. If she hid the truth, she misguidedly thought she could shield them from reality, so she told them Dad had suffered a heart attack.

But the one person she couldn't deceive was me. I arrived back from Australia that day, took one look at my father and knew exactly what had gone on. I was persuaded to go back to university, still worried about him but rationalising that my father had at least been able to talk to his doctor.

Mum and Dad made their peace, but deep down Mum was at her wit's end. She felt isolated and trapped. It was a living nightmare, struggling to keep from going under herself, and she had nowhere to turn for help. My parents were caught up in a cycle of codependency, despair and dysfunction.

In the 1970s New Zealand had one of the highest male suicide rates in the world. Its healthy outdoor image was at odds with the reality of hidden mental health problems, particularly prevalent in rural communities. There was one specialist clinic to treat depression, but it was hundreds of miles away from where we lived, and the shame of mental illness at that time prevented my father from seeking further treatment.

In her diary entry of 4 February, in a state of despair Mum wrote, *I don't think I can go on much longer like this.*

When I look back, I don't believe that we had more than our fair share of life's misfortunes. It just seemed to me that they all came at once when I was trying to make my own way in the world, and I found my salvation by escaping the family home as soon as I was old enough. Yet not once, despite the strain they were under, did Mum and Dad stop loving their children. Even though Mum's diary entry was her own cry for help, lurking within her was a strong character with a steely sense of resolve. By the following day she and Dad had somehow managed to pick themselves up again, and even drove 26 miles to Nelson to go out to dinner and the cinema.

CHAPTER 17
– FAMILY LIFE

By 1977, Dad was getting migraine-like headaches nearly every week. Non-migraine sufferers have asked me if there might have been another underlying cause to my dad's headaches. I can't be certain as MRI scans had only been invented that year, but what I do know is that Dad only got headaches when he was upset.

When given the opportunity, Mum embraced life to the full, but try as she might to lead her own life, she couldn't help but get dragged down by Dad's illness and her own punishing work schedule. By early March, she was exhausted and despondent. She had always suffered from emotional ups and downs and may have had undiagnosed Cyclothymic Disorder (severe mood swings), but the highs had mostly balanced out the lows – until she started taking mind-altering medication.

Dad had become tired of the hard physical work running an orchard and had come up with a plan to subdivide our land. He sold the business, but kept the house, garden and grazing land. Money, though, was a worry as he was only fifty and I was still a student.

Away from work, Mum kept herself busy by taking up hobbies. She loved classical music, show tunes and reading poetry, but to get herself out of the house she took up pottery and floral art. She felt though, that Dad had a tendency to undermine her.

He's always trying to rubbish any hobbies I have – always has done and that's why I haven't had any (or hadn't).

Mum was feisty and refused to allow Dad to walk all over her. She and Dad were polar opposites: Mum was outgoing and sociable, whereas Dad had become increasingly introverted. When she did manage to coax him out of the house to see friends, he enjoyed himself and forgot about his worries, and every now and again there would be glimpses of his young and carefree self. He liked to relax in front of the television watching British comedies. And if his favourites comedians, Tommy Cooper or Dave Allen came on, they were guaranteed to bring a smile to his face. But by 1977, there seemed to be precious little left to laugh about.

After Dad sold the orchard he came up with a new type of television aerial, and set up a small assembly plant to manufacture it. But he didn't have the expertise in marketing and distribution, and had to go into partnership. Like many business partnerships there were the occasional disagreements, and even though they were more petty squabbles than major conflicts, these upsets caused friction at home.

Dad didn't seem to have much enthusiasm for this new venture; in fact, he didn't have much enthusiasm for anything. When we owned the orchard, he'd had to put the effort in to motivate his staff, but while he was developing the aerial business, the only staff were Mum and me. For the rest of the time, Dad worked alone, lost in his thoughts.

I don't know what he thought about my sister graduating as an occupational therapist in March that year, but I hope it left him feeling a little less despondent. Mum, certainly was cheered by this, and was looking forward to celebrating with Susan the next time she came home. And to top it all, the day after graduation, much to Mum's delight, Susan announced that she had got engaged to her boyfriend, Paul.

On the morning of 29 March 1977, Mum slept in after her night duty then woke up feeling cranky and worried about Dad. He looked wrung out as he was working by himself and had a big order to fill. By the following day, he had another acute migraine attack and Mum had to give him another pain-killing injection. The next day he felt like a different person and was both loving and affectionate towards her.

But the change in mood didn't last as one of Dad's business partners phoned to say he couldn't meet up that day. He failed to turn up on Monday too, and in her diary, Mum accuses the two partners of stirring up trouble.

I hope they read this, and someone else does too. Up them!

She cheered up when Susan and I said we were coming home for Easter. Susan was bringing Paul with her and Mum wanted them to announce their engagement formally by putting a notice in the local paper.

Mum packed as much as she could into her days off. One time she even drove me the 500 miles to my university and then made the return journey on her own. After that four day trip she promptly went out socialising, but by the end of her hectic week she felt so faint that she had to rest.

Mum resented Dad's business partners for their inability to make firm plans and found it tedious, having to stay home waiting around for them. One Sunday, Mum wrote that it had been a *nice 'pest free' day* as neither of the two business partners had made an appearance. It probably didn't help that she had to do an extra night shift to cover for sick leave, as all this did was make her more tired and irritable. Her one-word entries for an entire working week read: *tired*.

The night before Mum's fifty-first birthday, 1 May 1977, there was a big storm. Gales and driving rain forced her to stay inside all day on her birthday, which she found frustrating. She couldn't even have a cigarette because she had a sore throat. To top it all, she was on night duty and she only had six birthday cards. Both Susan and Dad had forgotten.

First time for Ian.

Luckily her friends Bob and Peggy, who came round that Sunday, remembered.

The following Friday morning, she woke up feeling dopey.

Damn those Mogadon, etc. I think I'll stay awake all night and write letters.

By then her tablets had become a crux. And despite the remark that insomnia might have been preferable to pills, she carried on taking them.

The following Saturday Dad's two little nieces arrived to stay. Mum enjoyed having the children to visit, but she wasn't given time off work. When she had to rest, Dad pitched in to help. He did his best, but his depression had got the better of him and he was poor company. Mum took the girls on outings, but felt worn out, juggling night duty with the demands of looking after children.

On Monday 16 May, Dad's fifty-first birthday, it was cold and wet. I was home by then and cooked that night as Mum thought she was going down with 'flu. The next morning she was still feeling under the weather, but put in an effort for her nieces, as she didn't know when she'd see them again, as they were leaving for a new life in the UK.

On Friday, it was my eighteenth birthday. We didn't make much fuss about birthdays, but I got lots of cards, and Mum and Dad had already given me a coat as my present. Monday was Mum's last night on duty, but before she left for work she had a barney with Dad, who was in a belligerent mood. They had argued over me. Dad had wanted to drive me back to university and Mum had objected, saying I could fly back on my own. The next morning, before going to sleep, she took two powerful sedatives that combined two types of barbiturate. The brand she took was Tuinal, a drug so potent that it has since been withdrawn from sale in the United States. Mum only thought in the short-term, taking life one day at a time and not allowing herself to reflect on what the long-term side effects might be.

Those Tuinal certainly work – woke up at 4pm feeling stupid.

When she couldn't sleep after a night's work, she got up and picked apples or went for a walk to try to tire herself out. After dropping me off at the airport on the morning of Friday 27 May, she had planned an outing to take her mind off my leaving. But she couldn't go in the end as she felt too tired. On Saturday night she was called in to work at short notice, and she was too scared of her boss to say no. Exhausted after her shift, she went to bed at 8am on Sunday morning and slept until lunchtime, but woke up feeling out of sorts (it didn't help that it poured with rain all day). She fretted that her tiredness was due to anaemia, and gave herself a B12 injection. And to top it all, she felt unsettled as a friend had written with news that she was moving back to England.

While Dad was away on a business trip, my sister rang, inviting her up to Palmerston North. She felt that a trip away might do her good, but wanted to ask Dad first if he minded, but couldn't get hold of him. She decided to go anyway, and made the most of her little holiday. She and Susan went out for dinner and to the pub, where a man asked her to dance. I know she never told Dad that!

She flew home on a wet, cold Saturday morning and the little plane was buffeted by gales across Cook Strait. Dad was there to meet her, but something – she didn't know what – had upset him. Mum felt very deflated, tired and out of sorts after her trip, and her low mood impacted on her organ practice (she had just bought an electronic keyboard). To top it all, a window fell out of Dad's car.

Mum's trip away had left her wanting more and she

managed to persuade Dad to help her plan a trip to the UK for 1978. She was so fed up, she wrote this:

SUNDAY B. [Bloody] *SUNDAY*
Wanted to phone A[lison]*but Ian said best not to as I was so tired. I'm absolutely buggered tonight.*

By Tuesday, she was feeling more upbeat. Dad had told his business partners that he didn't want to commit to more than a three-year partnership, and even if going back to live in England was little more than a pipe dream, it meant that Mum didn't feel so trapped in New Zealand.

This makes me feel a lot better.

Feeling relieved, she gave her organ playing another go and was pleased with her efforts.

Can nearly play 'Fascination' without a mistake now.

At work the following night, Mum was pleased that her patient had a rapid delivery and the doctor on duty was able to get away early. On Thursday after her night shift, she took two barbiturates and a benzodiazepine and slept through until 8pm, but she felt guilty when she woke up as she'd left Dad on his own all day. On Friday, after another night shift, she wrote that she'd had a good sleep in the morning.

Ian in rather a grouchy mood. Can't blame him really. He doesn't like being on his own too much.

Saturday 25 June was dull and overcast, but Mum was cheered up by an invitation to a meal with her friends, Bob and Peggy. On Sunday, it rained all day, but Mum woke up in a good mood on Monday morning.

GOOD DAY. One of the best for ages. Both in good moods. No cross words.

On Tuesday, a big storm brought heavy rain. After the storm, Mum went up to the top paddock to check on our rescue pony, who my kind-hearted mother had saved from a callous owner, who had wanted to send Goldie to be slaughtered. Fortunately, apart from a torn rug, Goldie was fine.

Felt very tired but only took ½ a K.A.A.

My best guess is that this is shorthand for a Keep Awake pill – a stimulant, probably an amphetamine. It may even have been a diet pill, often used by non-dieters, such as students, cramming for exams. They too had nasty side-effects.

I was a casual user of prescription only diet pills for ten years, but finally quit them after a scare at an aerobics class. I had taken a pill with my meagre breakfast, then went and did vigorous exercise. Mid-class my heart started racing, and I felt like I was about to pass out. I rushed out of the studio, put my head between my knees, then went home and threw away all my tablets.

On Friday 1 July, it rained all day.

Felt so TIRED I could cry. Felt tired all day.

To cheer herself up she had her hair done, but she was struggling to write a letter to my sister. Susan was starting to assert her independence and Mum felt threatened by that. My sister wanted to travel, but first she had to find the money to buy her way out of a Hospital Board contract, as she'd been paid during training. Mum and Dad thought she was irresponsible, and said as much in the letter. On the same night that I rang home, complaining about my bout of ill-health, Susan rang, very upset by Mum's letter.

On Thursday, it was the seventh day of the seventh month of 1977.

Got up feeling very tired and grouchy towards everyone.

Mum was still cross with Susan for standing up for herself, and *for not really wanting to come home.* With too much to think about, she left it a bit late leaving for her evening class. As she drove out of the driveway and along the road beside the tidal inlet, she reached over for her glasses, knocking the steering wheel. The car veered off the bank, flipped over onto its roof, and then miraculously back onto its wheels. By then it had rolled into the inlet, but the tide was out – 7/7/77 was Mum's lucky day. She walked away unscathed without so much as a scratch, but as she walked up the drive in the dark, all she could think about was what Dad would say, and how much it would cost to repair the damage.

Dad had to find a way of getting the car out of the inlet, but he no longer owned a tractor so had to call the neighbours for help. It was winter, pitch black and the car was in sticky mud. And the tide was coming in fast. Just in the nick of time they pulled the car clear.

By Saturday, Mum had shrugged off her accident. On Saturday 16 July Dad had a migraine headache, and then I made things worse.

Phoned Alison – she said she spent $40 on a weekend skiing. Ian went to bed very fed up – at 9.30pm to be precise. He just can't take family upsets.

Even though there were no university tuition fees and I'd been awarded a government bursary, Mum and Dad were paying my rent and living expenses. Skiing to them was a luxury and they didn't approve of me spending money I didn't have. Later that year I flew up to Auckland to see Fleetwood Mac. I'd learnt my lesson by then and kept that one quiet.

Although no doubt disappointed with me, Mum and Dad seemed to be getting on better than they had in a long time. Mum enjoyed helping Dad out with the aerials and was making progress with her organ playing, and that winter she resumed her dream diary. She'd had a disturbing dream that Dad's business became so successful he had to employ dozens of people, and he was so busy he was never able to get away. But Dad was so ill by then that he struggled even to keep his modest business venture running. At 8.30am that morning Mum had to give him a pain-relieving injection for another migraine, and she was, as usual, complaining of being tired.

On Saturday 23 July she was feeling so down that she

struggled to make it out of bed and got up late. She was due to work that night, but rang a colleague and asked if she would cover her shift. Mum then rang her boss and said she had 'flu.

By that afternoon, she was feeling well enough to go socialising, but by the next morning her mood had fallen flat. She'd had a disaster trying to style her hair and hated the way it had turned out. She asked Dad to phone in sick on her behalf and say she couldn't work that evening, but not to tell the hospital what was really wrong with her.

She worked with Dad for five hours that afternoon, and for the following two days while the rain beat down on the shed roof. Mum had a music lesson to break the monotony, while Dad had such a bad migraine attack he needed another pain-killing injection.

Later that month my sister came home for a visit. She and Dad had a big row, but it seemed to clear the air, and Susan made baked jam roll for pudding, one of Dad's favourites, as a peace offering.

I returned home from university on a dreary Friday, where it rained non-stop, and as Mum noted in her diary, was a BAD DAY. Susan had broken up with Paul and decided to move to Australia. Mum was fond of Paul and disappointed with my sister for wanting to go abroad.

By Tuesday morning, it was my turn to be in Mum's bad books.

I was woken up by A nearly knocking the door down with a cup of tea. I couldn't tell her off.

This was the only way I knew of waking Mum up as gentle knocks didn't work. My biggest fear was that one day she wouldn't answer at all. And I suppose by then I was sick of having to creep around the house. We would generally let Mum sleep in until 9.30am on non-working days; if we got her up any earlier, we'd pay for it for the rest of the day. Susan and I went shopping while Mum stayed behind and made bread. By the time we got home, she was in an awful mood – my fault for waking her up too early.

Horrible to everybody. Could be time of the month, but think it's the weather.

Mum's bad mood impacted on Dad as he got another migraine headache. He needed two more painkilling injections as the headaches lasted all week.

On Saturday 13 August Mum and Dad took us out to dinner at the Rutherford, the only fine dining restaurant in the area. Susan and I got very excited and dressed up for the occasion, but Mum got cross with us for ordering what she called *revolting looking and very expensive cocktails*. She was out of sorts as she had to work that night. I used the occasion to finally tell my family the truth about how badly I was doing at university, which didn't go down well. Then my sister was in Mum's bad books for making an expensive phone call to her ex-boyfriend.

By the end of the week, Susan and Mum had come to some sort of truce, and by the weekend, she'd recovered her good humour. We enjoyed a long walk on the beach with the dog, bought fish and chips so Mum wouldn't have to cook, played mini-golf, and on Saturday night, persuaded Mum and Dad to take themselves off to the cinema.

Susan and Mum had one final bust-up, (this time over the ownership of some clothes), before Susan flew to Sydney. While Mum was driving home from the airport, Dad was having trouble with his new assistant, and was so stressed out, that when she got back she had to give him one of her anti-anxiety tablets.

My parents felt so empty and sad that Susan had gone that on Friday evening they drove 15 miles to see their friends, Bill and Hazel. Then we had friends coming round that weekend, and by Saturday night the mood in the house had lifted. Dad was cracking jokes and Mum was her sparkling social self. I was glad to see them both happy, but on Monday I was due to return to Dunedin, and Mum was anticipating feeling down when I'd gone.

Big gloom day for me I expect as I have a free week. It's always the same. I'm never off when they are here.

In the end, I left the following morning, catching a direct flight at 11am. I phoned my parents that evening to say I'd arrived safely.

Miss her very much.

Felt terribly flat. Ian had one of his weekly sinus attacks [migraine] *so I had to be very careful what I said. We ended up having a row as usual, saying our whole marriage was a disaster, etc.*

Mum went to mass that evening. She did occasionally find solace in religion, but the heating wasn't working in the church and all she could think about was how cold she was. I don't know what it was that set them off, but that night my parents were upset by a programme on TV or radio.

I burst into tears when they played the 'March' by the Royal Marines, and Ian cried his eyes out when the two kids were so appreciative. What a cheerful pair we are. I suppose we'll get over it.

Mum pulled herself together in time for her night shift and left home at 11.30pm. It was a long night. She supervised a difficult birth and felt wrung out, then drove home carefully early Sunday morning as the road was slippery and the ground was blanketed in a thick white frost, which for spring was unusual. After sleeping until the afternoon, she got up and took the dog to the beach. She struggled through work until Wednesday morning.

All unsettled cos I've got to do the fourth night. It nearly kills me – and Ian.

I woke him up. Hope he'll be OK for the Friday Ball. Took 20mls (Tricloryl) + one blue and one red + one-and-a-half Mogadon.

Mum thought that by cutting her tablets in half, she was

in control. But the dangerous cocktail of benzodiazepines and barbiturates gave her a fitful sleep and left her feeling groggy and desolate.

Very depressed when I got up.

It must have been quiet at work that night as she had time to write in her diary.

Felt awful, but now feel OK at 2am and it's my last night anyway (till next week). Wonder how long I can stick four nights.

On Friday night, it was the Fruitgrowers' Ball. Mum was really looking forward to it, but she wasn't holding out much hope that they would go. She expected that either she would be too tired or Dad would get a sinus attack.

Ian did get another sinus attack. Needless to say I made him go to bed, have an injection and 1 red bomb. I left him sleeping and went to have my hair done. He woke up at 6pm – very thirsty but okay.

One red bomb had knocked Dad out cold for the day. Mum was half his size, yet regularly took two to three times that dose. For once, Mum's high-risk treatment seemed to work and Dad felt well enough to go to the ball.

Had a marvellous time at Ball.

Rather rashly, Mum had promised our neighbours that she and Dad would go climbing with them that weekend. It was thirty years since she'd gone near a mountain, and they were going up Mount Arthur, 1,500 feet higher than Scotland's Ben Nevis. But it was too late to back out.

Gawd! It was awful. I nearly died of fatigue on the way down.

It took her three days to recover.

Had to take a keep awake [amphetamine] *– nearly a whole one.*

The weekend got off to a bad start as Mum had a row with Dad's assistant, David, and he stormed out. To cheer herself up, she invited friends round for supper and cooked them roast beef and Yorkshire pudding, even though she didn't have much confidence at cooking.

Susan phoned home that week, reversing the charges. Mum timed the call.

Not a very satisfactory conversation. I was cross with her. She caught me at a bad moment.

Had a few words with Ian. He said I was making a big fuss over nothing. He doesn't have to try and sleep on a lovely sunny day.

On Friday after her night's work Mum came home and had just got to sleep when she was woken up by a delivery van.

More words with Ian. This time I AM going to resign – definitely. This is not worth it. It's ruining our marriage and my health.

Mum knew what night duty was doing to her health. But it's taken until now for neuroscience to prove it. Psychologist Professor Phil Tucker, speaking on the radio, said recently that for every ten years of night shifts the brain ages another six-and-a-half years. (Source: *The Night Shift*, BBC Radio 4, 2015). Back then there was nowhere Mum and shift workers like her could turn for help.

Saturday got off to a shaky start.

Had a music lesson – absolute disaster. I made hundreds of mistakes and can't use the pedals. I hate them.

Still, she didn't have time to dwell on her less than perfect playing as I was coming home and she drove to the airport to meet me. She must have had some time off as on Monday night she got to sleep at about 1am and slept right through until 10 the next morning.

On Tuesday, she worked in the shed.

Didn't feel 'switched off' at all due to only 1 Mogadon.

When Mum was desperate for sleep, she would take one tablet. If that didn't work, she would take a barbiturate, which made her feel like a zombie when she woke up. On

Saturday night, Mum went to work and plucked up the courage to talk to her boss about resigning.

Told Sister H I couldn't go on much longer doing Night Duty.

Nobody at the hospital took her concerns about her hours seriously, so her only option was to give up. And instead of being able to leave within the month of her statutory notice period, her boss put pressure on her to work for a further six weeks. But Mum knew this would cause tension at home.

Hope Ian doesn't mind as there are two lots of four nights after this one.

I left to go back to Dunedin on the Monday. Thursday dawned, and faced with another four nights on duty looming, Mum was in despair. But Friday night at work was quiet and she had time to write a long letter and reflect.

Spent a long time thinking about whether I should give up or not. I get so involved, I wonder if I could continue until January and then see.

Mum received two letters, one from her mother and one from Susan, on the last day of October, then Susan rang with good news that night. To Mum's delight, she'd had three job offers, all of which had excellent prospects. Mum went to mass on All Saints Day, 1 November, but came back feeling wiped out. She went to see her GP and he prescribed a fortnightly Vitamin B12 injection. I returned home in early November after my exams, the same day as my father collected his new car.

Saturday night was quiet for Mum at work, but there were a lot of newborns that week. When one cried, it set the rest of them off. Then on Monday night an anxious first-time father made Mum call the duty doctor out twice, both of which were false alarms. She finished her night shift after escorting a mother with a premature baby on a 60 mile round trip to Nelson hospital.

I left home in the second week of November to move to Wellington. I had switched to an arts degree and was making a fresh start in a new city. Dad was worried that I wouldn't get a job at the end of it, so to appease him I enrolled for a law paper too. Back at home, Mum organised a dinner party on Saturday night for friends she was in awe of, and she and Dad spent ages cleaning and tidying.

We had the house looking spotless. Ian cleaned the windows. I shampooed all the carpets, made a rush out to Kina and did a nice floral arrangement. We had goulash (Coleman's Casserole) and [frozen] *mixed veges, baked jacket potatoes, broccoli. I only had one small gin. The secret of being a good hostess is to stay sober. Very nice evening. We really like them, and they us, I'm sure, as they wouldn't have come otherwise.*

The next week started well. Mum went shopping in Nelson and blew her budget on sheet music and new shoes, but by midweek Dad had got another bad migraine and she had to give him a pain-relieving injection. Mum then got a letter from Susan saying that she wasn't coming home for Christmas, which upset her. Luckily, Saturday night at work was quiet and Mum managed to write a couple of letters. She was grateful as she had to leave Dad at home ill in bed, and before she'd left she had given him another injection.

Had two phone calls – one from Alison – the big spender – nice to hear from her. Then Susan phoned out of the blue. She sounded a bit funny. She's a bit mad, but is happy and NOT on drugs – I don't think.

I laughed when I read this. Mum had got the measure of me, but was completely wrong about Susan. The only person regularly taking drugs was Mum herself.

On Tuesday 6 December Mum flew to Wellington to visit me as I was feverish. I was too ill to meet her at the airport, so she took a taxi straight to my flat and we had a very relaxed evening. Poor Mum had to sleep on the couch in my sleeping bag, but luckily she had a good night. When I woke up the next morning I'd lost my voice, so Mum took me to see a doctor who diagnosed laryngitis and glandular fever.

Mum enjoyed herself on Thursday, although she complained she'd done too much walking. But by then she was sick of sleeping on my couch and moved into a motel. Then I dragged myself out of bed so that we could go out for dinner. I was very grateful to have her there.

Had a very gay time dancing to Ian's favourite tune 'Going to Rio'.

But the good times didn't last. My exam results arrived later that month, and according to Mum, I had failed miserably in all of them. She got that news on a Saturday, worked that night and then went straight to mass, no doubt to pray for me.

I flew home for Christmas from Wellington on Friday 23 December. Luckily we'd been invited to spend Christmas Day with friends, so there could be no awkward conversation about my results to spoil the festivities. On Boxing Day, Mum and I went to see friends, but Dad cried off, claiming he was feeling tired, brought on, no doubt by his depression.

On Thursday night at work, there were no deliveries or babies to look after and Mum and her colleague made the most of their light workload.

On New Year's Eve we were invited round to our Scottish friends for a Hogmanay party where there was even a bagpiper.

Ended up Scottish country dancing. Did a hilarious 8-some. Very pleasant New Year's Eve. A good start for 1978.

CHAPTER 18
– DEATH IN PARADISE

I was home for a month in the summer of 1978. We had been united in grief, saying a tearful goodbye to our cat Basil, whose sweet and loving nature had made him, in my eyes, an honorary dog. When I left on Tuesday 24 January, the day got off to a bad start as Mum had to get up at 7am to take me to the airport. Then I couldn't get on the flight, so we had to come home again, and Mum had a big row with Dad.

By then it was 77 degrees. Mum and I headed off to the beach for a swim before she had to drive me back to catch a later plane. By the time Mum got home, Dad was in the middle of another migraine attack and she had to give him an injection.

Mum slept in, swam and visited friends for the remainder of that week. One day she got up at 1pm and berated herself for sleeping in so late. Even though it made her feel sick with exhaustion, she'd stuck with her job, I think to get her away from the stifling atmosphere at home, but she woke up feeling awful on the Saturday morning when she was due to work. She rang in sick and told the Sister she had a tummy bug, then wrote in her diary that she didn't feel guilty about lying.

Easter was early that year and Mum cheered up when she found out that we were all coming home for the holiday. It passed amicably enough, although Mum got cross with me for arranging to see friends without getting Susan invited.

There were three events in 1978 that had a major impact on our lives, the first of which was that my grandmother's best friend died at Easter. Her death left a huge hole Ciss's life, second only to when she'd lost Don. While Brownie was alive, Mum had no need to worry about her mother back in England. It had always been Mum and Dad's plan that when Ciss was too old and frail to look after herself, she would come to live with us. Although my grandmother was still in good physical health, she felt that there was nothing left for her in Ferring. The time had come to move to New Zealand.

Back at home, Mum was at her lowest ebb. She was expecting to work on Friday 14 April, covering for a colleague, so she slept all day, but at the last minute she was stood down. Because she was worried she wouldn't sleep that night, she dropped in to see the chemist and persuaded him to give her two barbiturates. By Sunday morning, the side-effects made her feel even worse as she couldn't seem to stop crying. Somehow she managed to pick herself up and took herself off to see friends, but on Monday her mood was low again. When she phoned me that night, I could tell by the tone of her voice that something was wrong, but I didn't know how to help her.

Mum had to be strong for her mother's sake, just as she had done as a girl when they had been stuck in South Africa with no money. She told Ciss to hang on, that they would get to England as soon as they could, then drove to the travel agent. While she was in Nelson, she went to see another doctor who gave her more blue pills. Her own GP was no longer prescribing her all the drugs she wanted, so it had to be another doctor who was prescribing her the amphetamine and barbiturate combination, Drinamyl.

Mum picked herself up and helped Dad make aerials,

then went to the hairdresser's. I phoned up that evening, and this time we had a proper conversation as she remarked in her diary that I sounded happy. Mum was right in the middle of her four night shift, but after work on Friday night she couldn't go straight to bed as Dad had an urgent bulk order of aerials. She helped him from 8.30am until 1.30pm, then had a shower and got herself to bed, taking two barbiturates and two benzodiazepines to help her sleep. They knocked her out, as she slept right through to 6pm when she got up to make supper.

I rang home again that evening and offloaded my worries onto my mum. I certainly picked my moment! After comforting me, she had to drive to work. The next morning she came home and had a short sleep before getting up to give Dad a pain-relief injection for his migraine. The stress of the last minute order had set off another attack, but they still needed to pack up the aerials, which would take them all afternoon.

To cheer herself up, Mum planned a dinner party on Saturday night to celebrate her fifty-second birthday. There were eight round the table for shrimp cocktail and roast lamb. She felt worn out before the guests arrived, but perked up and managed to enjoy her own party. On her actual birthday, 1 May, she received just three cards. Susan and I hadn't managed to get it together to send her a card on time, and my brother, who did remember to call, had left it rather late. By then she was feeling hurt, and in her diary she called us a *lousy lot*. She was right.

To top it off, her management had put in a new system at work, and the midwives on duty were told they were no longer able to take turns to rest when they weren't busy.

This was her diary entry for Tuesday:

Am handing in my resignation tonight and Sister H can get someone else. Threw a terrible 'wobbler' and rang and said I had gastric flu.

Mum was in such a state she couldn't face going to work on Wednesday night. She promised Dad that this time she meant it and would resign, so he phoned her boss and pretended that she was sick. By the next morning she'd perked up, but the Sister had already found cover, so for once Mum was able to go to bed at a normal time. She slept for twelve hours.

Dad, meanwhile, was trying to persuade his business partners to increase the price of the aerials, but they fell out over it. Dad was in a bad mood the next day and blamed Mum, who was by then under such pressure that she had to go to the GP for a medical certificate, for causing the argument.

Mum only had one more month left at the hospital, but she wanted to leave on good terms. Thursday 15 June 1978 was her last ever shift at Motueka Maternity Hospital. She highlighted it in her diary with an exclamation mark.

Now that work was over, Mum was able to throw all her energy into her trip. Friends in Malaysia had invited her to stay on her way to England, and she was very excited to hear from them. And then I came home for a few days to say goodbye to my parents and collect my car.

On Thursday 13 July Mum flew to Wellington on the first leg of her journey. We had a lovely dinner out together that night, and the next day she flew to Australia to see my sister. After a lively night out in Sydney she managed to lose all her travel documents in a taxi. Luckily, the taxi driver handed them in to the police.

On Monday, Mum flew to Singapore.

Exhausted. Took 2 Tuinal (I think). The room was going round and round.

To me, that diary entry marks a turning point. Mum had told herself she needed the drugs to do her job, but now that she'd given up work, it seems she needed them in order to function. The next morning, with a hangover from the barbiturates and jet lag, she struggled to get up and felt dopey all day. She spent the day quietly at the hotel and had a swim in the pool. The next day was no better. In fact, by then she was feeling worse. She thought she'd caught a bug, but it may have been side-effects from the drugs.

Mum felt too ill to travel, so she got in touch with her friends and stayed an extra night in Singapore. She then had to get up at 6am to catch the train to Malaysia the next morning, but once she was on the train, she realised she'd left her two coats behind. She was furious with herself, but more worried about telling Dad.

As soon as she arrived she was swept up in a whirlwind of activities and thoroughly spoilt. She played golf, went swimming and was treated to meals out, and on the Saturday night there was a big party as Mum's hosts were celebrating two birthdays. While in Malaysia, she consulted a doctor about her tummy bug, but no matter how hard she tried to persuade him, he flatly refused to give her any more Soneryl.

Mum left Malaysia on 1 August to meet Dad in Singapore. Dad felt he could not go back to Malaysia as he'd never got over the shame of being kicked out of the job he loved, and ten years after he'd left, he'd been sent a retrospective tax demand from the Malaysian authorities. They had changed their tax laws, and his tax-free redundancy pay-off was tax-free no more.

My parents' reunion was a miserable one. On Wednesday, they had their first row of the holiday.

Terrible. Ended up with our usual rows about the same things. Told him about my coat. That should make his day. Why is he such a misery when I want to enjoy myself?

In their twenty-five years together they had coped with civil war, redundancy, running a business and raising three children. But the one thing they couldn't seem to survive was marriage.

Mum and Dad flew to England and stayed with Ciss in Ferring. On their first weekend, their friends threw a party in their honour. Mum and Dad were so skilled at keeping up appearances that no one would have known anything was amiss.

Dad soon got on with preparing his mother-in-law's house for sale. The first job was to put up a fence, but the next door neighbour objected.

Much unpleasantness all round. He got a migraine in the end.

By then Mum knew she was running low on barbiturates. As the doctor in Malaysia had refused to give them to her, she had to find a compliant one in England. During a routine enquiry about a blood test, she seized her opportunity. The GP did as he was asked and wrote her a prescription for Soneryl.

Mum used their visit back to England to catch up with as many friends as she could. Her best friend, Vicki, lived in Sussex, and Mum would go over there when she could, sometimes staying over. Mum had forgotten how congested the roads were in England and had a stressful visit to Brighton, which she found very crowded and tiring.

The rest of her time she spent with Ciss. Ciss's house had three viewings and was sold in five days, which was the second significant event of 1978. To celebrate, Dad took Mum and Ciss out to Worthing where they had a big spending spree. With one less worry, my parents began to enjoy each other's company, and despite all that life had thrown at them, they remembered that they really did still love each other. They packed as much socialising into that weekend as they could, driving up to Surrey to see friends from the Malaya days and visiting London to see Mum's Aunty May.

There were errands to run and last minute jobs around the house, but by midweek my parents both felt ill. Mum was convinced she was anaemic and Dad had a sinus attack in the middle of Wednesday night. He had already been to the GP who had given him pain-killer tablets, which seemed to do the trick.

Because it was high summer when the sea was at its warmest, Mum managed to get in a couple of swims at the beach, but the beneficial effects didn't last. On Thursday she had a blood test.

Hope it shows how anaemic I am. I really can't cope without B12.

Mum could be a bit of a hypochondriac, but she was right. It turned out that she had pernicious anaemia. After the blood test Dad took her out for what she called a *proper lunch*: fried scampi and salad. That night she wrote this in her diary:

Wish I'd hear from Alison at least.

I had assumed (wrongly as it turned out) that Mum would be so busy seeing all her friends that she wouldn't have time to miss her children.

On Saturday Dad and Mum were getting on well together. Dad was buoyed up following a meeting about a potential export opportunity for his aerials.

On Wednesday, Mum took Ciss to have her vaccinations and got back to find Dad in a bad mood. He was ruminating about a letter Susan had written to them. Susan had been trying to reassure them that all was well and she was loving her new life in Sydney, but Dad had misread it. He fired off a reply, telling my sister that not only did she have 'pie in the sky ideas', but she was never to try to exert her influence over me. It is a testament to her strength of character that Susan kept that letter a secret from me for thirty-five years. And far from driving a wedge between us, it brought us closer.

After a month cooped up in the same small house as her mother, Mum was starting to get cabin fever. Dad had to take her out to the local pub for a beer. She liked the atmosphere there and was looking forward to time away in Bournemouth with friends, but even this didn't seem to lift Dad's low mood. Their friends, who had always lived in some style, had recently moved into a wing of a stately home. Mum revelled in the luxury of staying in a castle, but Dad was too downhearted to enjoy it.

They returned to Ferring a week later, and in her diary entry for Monday, Mum wrote that Dad's low mood had begun to have a negative impact on Ciss. My grandmother may have been still grieving for Brownie, or maybe she was having second thoughts about moving in with Mum and Dad. She'd lived in Ferring in her own little house for over ten years, and now she was giving up her independence to live with her daughter in a country where she had no friends of her own. It must have been overwhelming.

On Tuesday Mum sent flowers to her hosts and then went to see the GP and persuaded him to give her more barbiturates. On Wednesday morning she was woken early by the postman with an official letter from the New Zealand Government. Being the methodical person he was, Dad had already spoken to immigration. As a dependent relative, Ciss would be granted residency, and all they were waiting for was the formal offer, which came a week later. But for some reason, this upset Mum – perhaps because it meant they were cutting yet another tie with England.

In a bad mood tonight. Very horrible to Ian. Said I didn't want to go back to NZ at all. Said I'd rather be dead, etc. Ended up taking two Soneryl and gave him one.

The following day Mum felt much better after a restful night, but now it seemed it was Dad who couldn't get to sleep.

He won't go to the doctor for more pills.
Was horrible to Ian. He had a violent vomiting attack.

It was mid-September and my parents had just three

weeks left to see friends and family as well as pack up Ciss's house. They drove to see Ian's sister Gill and her girls in Bedford, then went via London to see Mum's aunt and got stuck on the South Circular. It was hard saying goodbye, and it was a long drive home to Ferring.

Left Gillian in tears. Felt so sorry for her. Very harrowing for us all.

On the Saturday after the trip Mum woke up very late. She felt terribly tired and tense, ending up with a bad headache and spending the afternoon in the garden, soaking up the sun. Deciding it was anaemia that was making her tired, she gave herself a Vitamin B12 injection.

On Monday 25 September, with the completion date looming, Mum and Dad had to sort out the house. It was a very busy day for Dad as there were so many things to organise. To help out, Mum put adverts for used furniture in the local Post Offices, but back at home, there was trouble brewing between her and her mother. Ciss found her daughter exasperating and couldn't seem to get through to Mum that she couldn't have everything she wanted in life. And the one thing that Mum seemed to want more than anything was to live in England. No wonder Ciss was feeling so apprehensive about her decision to move to New Zealand.

On Tuesday they went up to London to see Dad's aunt and uncle and had a lovely day with them. They were taken out to lunch and talked non-stop until mid-afternoon, but Mum had too much wine at lunchtime and had to take four headache tablets before they could travel back to Ferring.

The next day Mum got up very late, then she and Dad went to Worthing.

Had a big row with Ian. He ended up walking back to Ferring from Worthing. I was very sorry afterwards and wrote him a letter of apology. We were both very tired.

Dad had a migraine attack after the upset of the day and

had to have a pain-relief injection. The following day, Mum went to see her doctor.

Had to ask him for more Soneryl tablets. He was terribly kind to us both – marvellous man.

By Saturday, Mum was feeling hemmed in and was desperate to get out of the house.

Felt terribly tense. Must phone Vicki tonight or I'll go mad. Went into Goring to shop. Ian caught me shoplifting some Danish butter. Felt very ashamed.

Mum only ever shoplifted for kicks when she was away from home. She felt elated when she got away with it, but deeply ashamed when she was caught. Mercifully, when she was stopped, the store detectives knew the difference between a professional thief and an amateur thrill-seeker, and treated her with compassion.

That Monday, 2 October 1978, Mum spent the day with Vicki and her children. She went to bed at a respectable time, but ended up taking two-and-a-half barbiturates and one benzodiazepine to get herself to sleep. On Friday, Mum and Dad went to London on the train to meet up with old friends and had a fantastic reunion, talking non-stop. They got back to Ferring that evening and arranged to see Vicki one last time, and also Mum's cousin and his family. On Sunday night, after another old friend had phoned, Mum and Dad held each other, reaffirming that despite all their ups and downs they still loved each other.

Their time in England was drawing to a close. On Monday 9 October, while Mum was packing and last-minute shopping in Worthing, Dad came down with another migraine. With all the turmoil and Dad's illness, they had forgotten to organise a farewell for Ciss, but fortunately a friend had arranged a surprise party. Another friend came to visit that week, and he and Mum were able to go out together for a long walk while Dad stayed in bed.

On Thursday 12 October, Mum, Ciss and Dad left 2

Ferring Close for good and stayed for two nights at a local hotel. On Saturday, they went to say goodbye to friends, before catching a night flight from Heathrow. The original plan to fly via Hong Kong and stop off for a few days had been abandoned. Instead they flew straight through to New Zealand, a punishing twenty-four-hour journey.

They arrived in Auckland on Monday 16 October and flew to Wellington where we had a meal out together. Dad was quiet and withdrawn; something was troubling him, I could tell by the ashen look on his face. After dinner Dad handed me a cheque. And then his demeanour changed. It seemed as though he was putting his finances in order, and that by paying for my rent in advance, this was one more worry lifted from his shoulders.

The next day my parents and Ciss flew home. That night, Mum and Dad, still jet-lagged, had a terrible argument and Dad stormed off into the night. The next morning he was found dead in the orchard from gunshot wounds.

I was just a week away from taking university exams. Although I was offered internal assessment instead of having to sit an exam in some papers, the law department wouldn't budge. I had to take the exam if I wanted to get into the second year; entry was competitive, and the pass mark was 75%. As I'd taken the paper to please Dad, the least I could do was try to pass it.

I flew back from Dad's funeral to sit the paper, but when I sat down I was shaking so much I could barely write my name. I passed everything else, but failed law by a few marks.

I made a pact with myself that despite my grief, I was determined not to be a victim and allow Dad's death to pull me under. My coping mechanism was denial. Instead of taking time off to grieve, I threw myself into my summer job in Wellington.

Fortunately there was sufficient reasonable doubt over

the circumstances of Dad's death for the coroner to record a verdict of Accidental Death, which meant that Mum, who had been left with no income, was able to claim on Dad's life insurance policy. At first, we thought we might lose both parents as Mum felt so guilty and blamed herself, but she had to try to be strong for the sake of her children and her newly dependent mother.

But the strain did eventually become too much to bear, and in the early part of 1979 she took an overdose. A family friend, who had come over from England, was staying, and when Ciss went to wake Mum, there was no response. She called out, pleading with Mum to wake up, then tried the door. It was locked.

Our friend broke into Mum's bedroom and found her unconscious. They called the ambulance and she was rushed to hospital.

She came round, groggy and disoriented, and unable to understand what the drip was doing in her arm, she pulled the needle out. The nurse panicked, claiming Mum was making another suicide attempt, and being a weekend there was no specialist on duty. Before anyone knew what was happening, two doctors were summoned and had sectioned Mum under the Mental Health Act. She was sent to Ngawhatu Psychiatric Hospital for six weeks, admitted into the geriatric ward even though she was only fifty-two.

We were still struggling to cope with Dad's death, and it seemed to me that the authorities were trying to take our mum away from us too. They fobbed us off, telling us that the law was the law, so I deferred my degree and took a semester off, my sister resigned from her job in Australia, and we moved back home to be with our grandmother.

Every day for those six weeks we drove the 40 mile round trip to visit Mum in hospital. The hospital was at the end of an isolated valley, and the route was overhung by evergreen trees. I remember gripping the steering wheel a little tighter, telling myself I had to be strong for Mum's sake, as we turned off the main road and drove up the long, menacing driveway.

I had to hold my breath walking in as the stench of urine made me gag. The other patients, most of whom seemed to be in the grip of dementia, wandered around, crying or calling out to unseen demons. The only therapy the doctors seemed to dispense at Ngawhatu was yet more drugs, not exactly the treatment suitable for someone who'd tried to kill themselves with pills. Mum wasn't even given bereavement counselling.

As much as we hated going there, we were always reluctant to leave. A family friend, who came every week, was a former prisoner of war who had escaped from a notorious German camp. We joked about hatching a plot to spirit Mum out of there, and when we told her we got a smile out of her, the first one in months. Joking aside, had the psychiatrists tried to carry out their threat to give her ECT, I think I would have been there with a shovel, digging the escape tunnel myself.

I was scared of the men in their white coats and the power they wielded, worried that they might turn their attention to me and Susan and try to lock us up in their maximum security hell hole. When we had to leave Mum behind in the evening, all I could think of was how vulnerable she was in that place. My fears were well-founded. Although Mum was okay, in 2004, four patients took the hospital authorities to court alleging abuse.

After the longest six weeks of my life, Mum was finally allowed to return home, where she picked herself up again and began to enjoy life. She took trips, both in New Zealand and further afield to Australia and the UK, and along the way she continued to draw in yet more new friends, even having relationships with a number of men. She volunteered at Riding for the Disabled, joined a choir and the local amateur dramatic society, and got a great review in the local paper for her role in *The Pyjama Game*.

She lived in a community where kind-hearted people looked out for her. Her GP gave her a part-time job in his surgery, which gave her a sense of purpose. She and Ciss rubbed along together, even though they sometimes got on each other's nerves.

Then my grandmother, who had barely had a day's illness in her life, needed a minor operation. She was terrified of hospitals, and tragically she died in Nelson Hospital of post-operative complications.

When she was alive, Mum had taken her mother for granted. But it had been Ciss who had got Mum out of bed every morning and was the only one who could tell her off for "taking all those damn pills". Without Ciss, Mum had no one to act as her conscience and her addiction began to spiral out of control. Her job at the surgery gave her access to drugs in ways that she never imagined, and even though her doctor tried to wean her off prescription drugs, she was by then both physically and psychologically dependent.

In 1992, it was alleged that Mum had been forging prescriptions. To avoid a prosecution, she checked into New Zealand's only rehabilitation clinic, Ashburn Hall. Mum was being asked to take responsibility for her addiction for the first time in her life, but by then she was sixty-six.

And then, in a bizarre and dangerous experiment, the hospital began to withdraw all her drugs. When I spoke to a specialist in the treatment of older patients, he advised me that given her long term history of dependency, the withdrawal should have been far slower – a period of years and not weeks. And the safe option would have been to keep her permanently on a low dose of medication. The physical and psychological side-effects terrified her and gave her tremors and a compulsion to chain-smoke. She would light cigarette after cigarette, which was very distressing to witness.

Mum was required to take part in group therapy sessions, but she was from a generation that hid their feelings and kept secrets and she found the sessions patronising and simplistic. She was clever and ran rings round the mental health workers, playing along and giving the answers she thought they wanted to hear. All she wanted was to get out of there, but they told her that she was resistant to therapy, which was true. Mum didn't want to give up drugs as not one of those psychiatrists could offer her any real alternative that numbed her pain.

After three months in Ashburn Hall, she seemed to have reached a plateau and wasn't getting any better, and I worried that she would become institutionalised. If I flew out to New Zealand and brought her home, I thought she would soon revert back to her former self, but I realised when she would barely sit in her seat on the flight back to Nelson that perhaps I had made a mistake.

Mum was very agitated and I struggled to deal with her changed behaviour. Our roles had reversed and I had become her carer. And I wasn't very good at it. The only time I could safely leave her on her own was when she was sleeping as she left lit cigarettes burning in ashtrays around the house. Nicotine was the only drug available to her, and she used it to counteract the terrible withdrawal symptoms from the benzodiazepines and barbiturates.

One time I was invited out to a friend's house for coffee and I sneaked out early, leaving Mum asleep. It was such a relief to get out on my own, away from my caring duties, that I stayed out for longer than I should. When I got home late that morning, I was worried sick that there would be lit cigarettes lying around the house. If the house had caught fire and she had died, it would have been all my fault, but to my relief, all was quiet.

Mum was curled up, still asleep, lying there so peacefully that I wished at that moment she would never wake up.

But wake up she did, and from then on I struggled with my responsibilities. I was very grateful to all her old pals, who rallied round as soon as they knew she was back and called in to check on us from time to time.

Between us, my sister and I hatched a plan to bring Mum back to the UK, where we both lived, to see if we could find a way to look after her there. I stayed on for another few weeks, and then Susan flew out with her children. How my sister, with two young children and Mum in tow, coped on the return journey, I'll never know. The first flight was twelve hours, and then they had to change planes at the halfway point. Then it was another twelve hours before they got back to England.

Mum went to live with Susan's family, but she kept running away. She was admitted to a local care facility as a temporary stop gap, until she ran away from that as well. We researched all the care homes up and down the country, but none of the good ones took patients with mental health issues.

With her own children to look after, my sister had too much to deal with. I received a call at very short notice that Mum was on her way up to stay with me, but I had just signed a contract agreeing to deliver a TV programme in three weeks' time. And I was travelling between Liverpool and Edinburgh where we were filming while scouting locations, organising interviewees, hiring crew and equipment and finalising the script.

I managed to find an agency that would come to the flat every day and look after Mum while I went to work. They didn't normally care for older people with psychiatric care needs, but they could hear the desperation in my voice. Mum really liked her carer, who was brilliant with her. She got Mum to help prepare the evening meals, and that made Mum feel needed.

By then, Mum been put on new meds by her UK doctor.

He'd prescribed what was then a new form of anti-depressant – touted as the safest non-addictive one on the market – the most well-known brand of which was Prozac. Unfortunately, it was the wrong drug for her as Mum suffered some nasty side-effects. It gave her sleeping difficulties, anxiety, nervousness and restlessness – disastrous for someone withdrawing from barbiturates and benzos.

I made an arrangement to send Mum back to my sister's after the weekend as I was due up in Edinburgh the following week. Although I wasn't very happy about Mum travelling on her own for five hours on the train, I couldn't see how I could get everything ready for the film shoot, drive from Liverpool to Devon and be back in time for filming. And Mum had made the train journey up to me without incident.

On the Sunday we spent a lovely day together, driving out to North Wales and having lunch at a pub which overlooked the sea. Mum seemed to me to be happier than she'd been in a long time. On Monday morning I took her to catch the 10am train, waved goodbye to her and went straight to work.

Less than an hour later she would be dead, falling from the train just outside Crewe. It was 19 October, two days after the anniversary of my father's death. I blamed myself.

We decided that we would fly Mum's body back to New Zealand so that she could be buried next to Dad and Ciss. Susan and I flew out together for the funeral. On my return I heard about a solicitor who was building a case against the rail operator over the safety of their trains' slam doors, which could be opened while a train was moving, or could fling open without warning if they hadn't been shut properly.

The solicitor agreed to represent us at Mum's inquest and to include our case as part of a class action against British Rail. I was astounded when I found out about the number of people who had died falling from trains and that the train doors might be faulty. British Rail's PR department had done such a fine job of hiding this news that the public knew nothing about it.

It was a David versus Goliath court case. Our lawyer worked out of a small room above a shop in a run-down shopping centre. British Rail employed the best legal brains money could buy. The stakes couldn't have been higher: the government was planning to privatise the railways, and the last thing they wanted was adverse publicity and an expensive refit of all their trains. They did everything in their power to blame the passengers, claiming that the train doors must have been left open deliberately by those intending to jump from the train.

Our side put expert witnesses on the stand who argued that the issue wasn't about whether the door had been left open, but that the company had a duty of care to ensure its doors were kept shut. We won our case. And although it was too late to save Mum's life, we would at least now prevent other needless deaths. Other families wouldn't have to go through what we did, and whenever I'm on a train waiting for the centrally locked doors to open, it reminds me of what we achieved.

* * * *

Even though she's been dead now for over twenty years, there isn't a day goes by that I don't think of Mum. It's the little things that set me off. Her favourite aria, 'The Pearl Fishers Duet', still has the power to reduce me to a blubbering wreck. But as much as I mourn her, I also think about how much she loved me.

When the letters and diaries were passed on to me, at first I was afraid to read them. I was curious to know what Mum had been like as a teenager, and, of course, to know more about her relationship with Steve, which was what compelled me to write about her life in the first place.

But in the process I found that I had to confront other more uncomfortable truths: the turmoil in my parents' marriage and the extent of her drug use. I had always wondered if there was more we could have done to help her. The psychiatrists at Ashburn Hall told me that Mum had been addicted to benzodiazepines, yet with all the reading I had done on their long term effects, nothing had prepared me for the shock of meeting her when I went to collect her from that clinic. It had been barely a year since we'd last seen each other, and she had seemed then still to be the capable and independent mother I knew.

Once I read Mum's diaries, the penny dropped. Neither we nor the clinic had anything like the full picture of what she had taken or for how long. And by the time she referred herself for help, the damage had already been done.

It is a common trait amongst children of addicts to have an overdeveloped sense of responsibility. I thought I could fix my mother. The truth was I couldn't, and that burden has been well and truly lifted from my shoulders now. I am thankful for the happy life I've been able to lead, and for all the support that I've received, and continue to receive, from my family.

I will be forever grateful to Mum and Dad for the sacrifices they made for their children, and for making me the person I am. Mum may have built her 'castles in the air', but at the same time she laid a solid foundation for her family's future. She would have been immensely proud of the achievements of her granddaughters and grandson, and would have loved that two of her grandchildren are now parents themselves.

Mum taught me to read by the age of three and instilled in me her love of words. I couldn't have become a writer without her.

(Figure 18.1 Alison, Hugh and Susan can be viewed in the gallery section of the website:http://www.lambertnagle.com)

ABOUT THE AUTHOR

Alison Ripley Cubitt is an author and screenwriter, and was the screenwriting columnist for nine years for *Writing Magazine*. She co-writes thrillers with Sean Cubitt as Lambert Nagle. *Castles in the Air* is her fourth book. Other books by this author:
Buying a House in New Zealand
Retiring to Australia and New Zealand (with Deborah Penrith)
Revolution Earth

Find out more about the author and future publications, including the Lambert Nagle short story, *Contained*, in *Capital Crimes* at:
http://www.lambertnagle.com
http://www.twitter.com/lambertnagle
https://www.facebook.com/alisonripleycubittwriter

ACKNOWLEDGEMENTS

I owe a great deal of thanks to those who advised me in the process of writing this book. I am particularly grateful to Dymphna Callery and Roz Morris for their help and advice on structuring the manuscript. A big thank you to Maureen Kermode, who gave me a lovely quote, and to Rona Morgan for her memories of Hong Kong. To Sue Clayton and Sean Cubitt for showing me the way into the story I was trying to tell. To Laxmi Hariharan who helped me clarify my reasons for writing the book. I am grateful to Sue and Terry Cubitt for assisting me with medical research.

Without the encouragement of my beta readers, Kate Jackson and Deb Rhodes, I doubt I would have got to the end. I was so close to the material by then that I had no idea whether or not it was even worth finishing.

Thank you to Jane Dixon-Smith, who is always such a pleasure to work with, for typesetting and layout; to Design for Writers for their beautiful cover design; to my copy-editor, Alison Jack, for not only challenging me to do better, but above all, for her patience and attention to detail.

And, of course, thank you to my sister Susan and my brother Hugh. And to Mum and Dad. I miss you both every day.

www.ingramcontent.com/pod-product-compliance
Lightning Source LLC
Chambersburg PA
CBHW020610300426
44113CB00007B/591